PRACTICING WITNESS

Practicing Witness

A MISSIONAL VISION
OF CHRISTIAN PRACTICES

Benjamin T. Conner

WILLIAM B. EERDMANS PUBLISHING COMPANY

GRAND RAPIDS, MICHIGAN / CAMBRIDGE, U.K.

Published 2011 by
Wm. B. Eerdmans Publishing Co.
2140 Oak Industrial Drive N.E., Grand Rapids, Michigan 49505 /
P.O. Box 163, Cambridge CB3 9PU U.K.

Printed in the United States of America

17 16 15 14 13 12 11   7 6 5 4 3 2 1

Library of Congress Cataloging-in-Publication Data

Conner, Benjamin T.
Practicing witness: a missional vision of Christian practices / Benjamin T. Conner.
            p.   cm.
Includes bibliographical references.
ISBN 978-0-8028-6611-0 (pbk.: alk. paper)
1. Theology, Practical.   2. Church work.   3. Church.
4. Dykstra, Craig R.   I. Title.

BV3.C645   2011
253 — dc22

                                                    2010054056

www.eerdmans.com

Contents

1. A Crisis in Ministry   1

2. The Missional Church and Missional Theology   11

3. The Practices in the *Practicing Our Faith* Conversation   43

4. Craig Dykstra's Conception of Christian Practices   69

5. Practicing Witness   87

   Epilogue: Amplifying Their Witness   109

   Bibliography   117

   Index   127

CHAPTER ONE

A Crisis in Ministry

At a camp designed in its program and property to accommodate adolescents with physical and intellectual disabilities, I was facing a crisis. James, a young man with Down syndrome, was inconsolably homesick. He had been crying on and off for two days already on this, the third day of a five-day camp trip and was at that moment sitting on the floor of our cabin with his arms wrapped around his legs hugging them and weeping copiously. It was my first year on staff with a ministry to such kids. The ministry creates community by recruiting and training leaders to be involved in their lives, by holding regular meetings during the school year, by teaming up with a local therapeutic riding center for a competition and excursion in the fall, and by taking a five-day camp trip together to a premier camping property in the summer. I was a seasoned youth minister with twenty years of experience working with kids. I had a master of divinity that suggested I had been prepared theologically to interpret and address the situation — in fact, at the time I was a defense away from a doctorate. Beyond such credentials, I had had the practical experience of raising my own four children to draw upon.

Still, I had nothing to offer.

Rather, I had nothing to offer James that in any way provided him comfort or perspective, and the entire cabin of campers knew it. One who particularly noticed my helplessness was another camper named Greg. As the consequence of a car accident just prior to his birth, Greg has cerebral palsy, an auditory processing disorder, and is learning disabled. He had seven major surgeries by the age of eight. Among the more significant surgeries, he had his ankles broken and his legs straightened and he had a selective dorsal rhizotomy to relax spasticity. He still moves awkwardly. Greg did not analyze the situation using the methods and techniques I had learned in seminary and then attempt to provide a solution to James's problem. Instead he took the initiative to sit calmly beside James, put his arm around him, and speak words of comfort and peace to him. Was it despite or because of his "limitations" that this young man was able to provide for James comfort that I could not? Was Greg uniquely gifted to be a nonanxious presence who could provide for James what James Loder described as "the self-confirming impact from the presence of the loving other"?[1] I believe Greg was adequately equipped and strategically placed by the Holy Spirit as a unique member of the body of Christ to minister to James. Greg bore witness to the alternate economy of the kingdom of God wherein the significance of one's contribution is not restricted by his or her marginality in society.

Greg changed, in that moment, my perception of disability, and my assessment of him shifted from a disabled kid for whom I was responsible to a partner in ministry. The impact of that experience required some time to pervade and reorient my approach to ministry to and with people with disabilities. Once again, Greg was there to help me. The same young man, James, was very upset at one of our regular club meetings because he had just lost his grandfather. This time I realized the contribution that our community could make in this situation, so we stopped our activity and had a time of prayer and encouragement for James. After a few minutes, I stood in front of the group and summed up our time with a prayer. When I concluded my prayer and opened my eyes, Greg was standing beside me. He had apparently worked his way to the front of the room while I was praying because he understood what I was still coming to terms with — that he has a contribution to make in the church. He was taking responsibility for the group — why wouldn't I have asked Greg to lead the prayer on behalf of his friend, or at least invited him to come up and pray with me? My time with the kids in our ministry has been filled with such experiences that have challenged my understanding of able and disabled, my

---

1. James E. Loder, "Negation and Transformation: A Study in Theology and Human Development," in *Toward Moral and Religious Maturity*, ed. Christine Brusselmans (Morristown, N.J.: Silver Burdett Co., 1980), 173.

notion of ministry and witness, and my fundamental understanding of faith and discipleship. Craig Dykstra's work and the insights of the *Practicing Our Faith* discussion have been very helpful in negotiating this paradigm shift.

Along with reforming my practice of youth ministry, my work with kids with disabilities has raised even more fundamental concerns about how we understand, affirm, and bear witness to the Christian faith. For example, it is the conclusion of the disability movement that people with intellectual disabilities are oppressed by societal structures and perceptions, and the Christian community has done little to address this injustice. The church has yet to become a space where people with disabilities have full access and inclusion.[2] Franklin is a young man whom I know who has autism spectrum disorder. How can the church make a space for Franklin's full participation as one who has severely impaired reciprocal interaction, has qualitative impairments in verbal and nonverbal communication, and exhibits unusual responses to the variety of sensory experiences? Is the way that my church defines faith, explicitly or in the implicit definition derived from how they talk about Christian discipleship, broad enough, comprehensive enough, nuanced enough to include Franklin? What about the profoundly disabled? Dykstra has given me a way to address faith formation that does not require Franklin to have communicative skills and cognitive abilities that he does not possess.

Even if Franklin never moves through discrete and incrementally advancing stages of human development, I can affirm that he can be engaged in a faith that can grow as he responds within the limits of his own capacities. The mission and ministry of Jesus provide the aims for Christian discipleship — the presence of certain capacities or structures does not ensure that Franklin will respond in faith. The lack of such capacities does not disqualify him from bearing the witness of the Spirit. Dykstra gives us a way to talk about discipleship not in terms of learning the right information or progressing through stages of faith, but in terms of creating spaces through Christian practices where Franklin can, through the Holy Spirit, experience, palpably feel, and respond to God. As someone who has been greatly impacted by mission theology, I also wanted to ensure that Franklin's responses to the love of God are recognized as intimately contextual;

2. Erik W. Carter, *Including People with Disabilities in Faith Communities: A Guide for Service Providers, Families, and Congregations* (Baltimore: Paul H. Brooks, 2007), 1-16.

a response to realities that, perhaps, because of our "ability" we are not immediately prepared to perceive. Franklin's contributions are essential to the community's understanding of the gospel and add an important intonation to our community's witness. Practical theology is the broader discipline that addresses such issues.

Practical Theology

Practical theology evaluates and guides Christian action in order to discern how to practice faith in ways that bear more faithful participation in God's ongoing redemptive work in the world in a particular social context.[3] I followed Rick Osmer's approach to practical theological reflection; that is, when hit with a crisis in the practice of ministry, ask the question, "What's going on?"[4] By engaging the situation through listening and attending to the people and events that brought about my ministry dilemma, I informally gathered information that helped me to discover the patterns and dynamics of a "new" situation that required an explanation and challenged me to revisit my theological understanding of some basic Christian assumptions. My experience in ministry to that point had not led me to consider faith in those with intellectual disabilities. I had no theological insight or paradigm for considering what discipleship might look like for a community that includes people with disabilities. My church did not include the variety of faith expression of those with intellectual disabilities in their witness, and I saw few opportunities or spaces for them to participate in the life of the community of faith.

Next, I asked the question, "Why is this going on?" During the next

---

3. John Swinton, a practical theologian at Aberdeen and a leader in the field of disability studies, offers a concise and mission-informed definition of practical theology: "A basic definition would be that practical theology is theological reflection on the praxis of the church as it strives to remain faithful to the continuing mission of the Triune God in, to, and for the world. Practical theology seeks to guide and critique ecclesial praxis as the church strives to fulfill its role as 'the hermeneutic of the gospel,' which is the place where the gospel is lived out and interpreted to the world through the actions and character of its participants." John Swinton, "The Body of Christ Has Down's Syndrome: Theological Reflections on Vulnerability, Disability, and Graceful Communities," *Journal of Pastoral Theology* 13, no. 2 (Fall 2003): 66-67.

4. This approach is found in a number of places, but most completely in Richard R. Osmer, *Practical Theology: An Introduction* (Grand Rapids: Eerdmans, 2008).

couple of years I sought conversation partners who could help me to address and explain the patterns and dynamics I have described above. This led me deeper into the literature about Christian practices, introduced me to the growing literature on adolescents with disabilities, and compelled me to interact with those specialists and parents who share life with adolescents with special needs. I found that many of the sociological reasons for the exclusion of those with disabilities from full participation in society were operative in the church as well and were not being challenged from a theological perspective.

Therefore, my next question was, "What ought to be going on?" With an eye on assessing and reforming my approach to discipling adolescents with special needs, and therefore my understanding of discipleship and ministry in general, I went back to my sources of theological insight for a context-dependent dialogue about making my praxis a more faithful Christian practice. This is the point at which I found Dykstra's work to be particularly informative, as I will explain in the coming chapters.

Finally, I considered the question, "How might we respond?" and promoted strategies of action and reimagination that challenged an area of praxis to include the contribution of the whole congregation. This included an approach to ministry with adolescents that focused each semester on participating together in one of the practices mentioned in *Practicing Our Faith*.[5] For example, for one entire semester the theme of hospitality shaped our activities, directed our Scripture lessons, guided our song selection, and served as an interpretive lens for our shared experiences. We learned together to encounter Christ, the true Host, in the strange other, to be servants to others, and we anticipated together the great eschatological banquet. The semester culminated in our kids hosting a group of adults with disabilities in a '50s dance. The kids prepared and served hors d'oeuvres, welcomed friends, and shared in word, deed, and song what hospitality meant to them.

Like all practical theology, however, this execution of the "pragmatic task" led to some new practical theological issues, and the process started all over.[6] In my research I came to believe that the practices discussion that

---

5. Dorothy C. Bass, ed., *Practicing Our Faith: A Way of Life for a Searching People* (San Francisco: Jossey-Bass, 1997). Their practices include honoring the body, hospitality, household economics, saying yes and saying no, keeping Sabbath, testimony, discernment, forgiveness, shaping communities, healing, dying well, and singing our lives.

6. The "pragmatic task" answers the question, "How might this area of praxis be

helped me to think theologically about discipling kids with disabilities needed to be reconsidered from the standpoint of the mission of the church. The new normative questions that were raised had a view toward addressing what I felt were deficiencies in the current discussion about Christian practices. The remainder of this book will explain how the practical theological method resulted in my reimagining Christian practices from a missional perspective. In a later book I will present how this practices approach to ministry with adolescents with special needs has resulted in an approach to ministry that I term "amplifying their witness."

Summary of the Project and Theological Foundations

The authors of *Practicing Theology* came together to reflect "on how the concept of practices that informs *Practicing Our Faith* might contribute to and be challenged by the work of systematic theologians."[7] In this book I will extend this discourse by reflecting on how the concept of practices articulated in *Practicing Our Faith* and given further theological clarity in *Practicing Theology* might contribute to and be challenged by the work of missional theologians. I will argue that an understanding of Christian practices that is informed by missional theology makes explicit and pronounced the witnessing aspect of Christian practices that is occasionally stated but undernourished theologically in the practices discussion. When one engages in Christian practices, one is practicing witness.

To make my case I will explore the following questions: What is missional theology? How have Christian practices been understood to this point? How might a missional theological perspective challenge the ways in which Christian practices have been conceived and practiced to this point? My hope is that this project will portray a collegial interchange that affirms the value in the conversations engendered by *Missional Church*[8]

---

shaped to embody more fully the normative commitments of a religious tradition in this particular context of experience?" It involves implementing strategies of actions for the sake of change. Osmer, *Practical Theology*, 3.

7. Craig Dykstra and Dorothy C. Bass, "A Theological Understanding of Christian Practices," in *Practicing Theology: Beliefs and Practices in Christian Life*, ed. Miroslav Volf and Dorothy C. Bass (Grand Rapids: Eerdmans, 2002), 18 n. 3.

8. Darrell L. Guder et al., eds., *Missional Church: A Vision for the Sending of the Church in North America* (Grand Rapids: Eerdmans, 1998).

and *Practicing Our Faith* and at the same time demonstrates the potential for a generative interaction that can materially advance present conceptions of Christian practices and missional theology.

I come at this task with several foundational assumptions and convictions. I am a Reformed theologian who believes strongly in God's prevenient grace and who emphasizes God's initiative in carrying out God's mission in the world. That is to say, my Reformed faith has been impacted greatly by the theological discussions of mission that have taken place in the ecumenical movement (particularly by the idea of *missio Dei*), by contemporary missiology, and by my experience in evangelistic ministry. As I will develop in the second chapter, these ideas and experiences have led me to embrace certain assumptions about the mission and calling of the church. Consequently, I agree with the great missionary scholar and practitioner Lesslie Newbigin with respect to the church's discipleship, that there is no participation in or union with Christ without participation in his mission in the world.[9] This is true for both able-bodied Christians and those with disabilities, intellectual or physical.

A second group of convictions that motivate this study cluster more specifically around Christian practices. While I believe there can be no understanding of Christian practices that does not account for the missional orientation of the Christian life, it is also true that a missional church that takes its calling seriously must attend to the practices that instantiate the life and witness of the community in a particular place. In my work with kids with disabilities, I found that participating together in Christian practices has provided a way beyond approaches to discipleship that socialize adolescents into visions of middle-class success and solid citizens or more evangelical approaches that focus on memorizing verses, a certain kind of Bible study, singing songs from a selection of emotive worship songs, and a program of trips and retreats. The first has never been an option for the kids I work with, especially those with more severe intellectual disabilities. The second approach often mimics culture but creates a Christian version of it that is so individualistic, abstract, and extracontextual that it is hardly relevant and fails to engage the culture to which it is called to witness in any meaningful way.

9. Norman Goodall, ed., *Missions under the Cross: Addresses Delivered at the Enlarged Meeting of the Committee of the International Missionary Council at Willingen, in Germany, 1952; With Statements Issued by the Meeting* (London: Edinburgh House Press, 1953), 190.

The practices discussion, on the other hand, has initiated a conversation that has addressed such issues as honoring the body, hospitality, household economics, saying yes and saying no, keeping Sabbath, testimony, discernment, forgiveness, shaping communities, healing, dying well, and singing our lives.[10] Furthermore, the practices discussion has given attention to specific Christian beliefs that are embedded in the practices and the means by which they are sustained and has, accordingly, initiated a revolution in how we understand Christian education. What remains to be drawn out, however, is a characterization of the practices of a church that is called, built up, and sent to participate in the ongoing mission of God in the world.

If, as the missional church discussion argues, the church is built up for the sake of following God in God's mission to the world, what should that reveal about the nature and purpose of practices of the faith? If, as Craig Dykstra suggests, faith is "appropriate and intentional participation in the redemptive activity of God," then how should such faith shape our understanding of the practices?[11] If, as Dykstra has written, mission is the purpose of Christian education and Christian education is mission, then what are the implications for the practices that constitute the curriculum?[12] What would it look like if mission were not thought of as the overflow or the result of practices but were, instead, the first thought that shaped the list of practices?

This process of understanding Christian practices as a way of sharing the life of discipleship with those with special needs understood through the perspective of missional theology has resulted in what I am terming "practicing witness."

Practicing Witness

All people have lenses through which they understand theological issues. I have already betrayed mine. In the next chapter I will elaborate on my missional theological lenses by offering a brief account of the conversa-

---

10. Bass, *Practicing Our Faith*.

11. Craig R. Dykstra, "What Is Faith? An Experiment in the Hypothetical Mode," in *Faith Development and Fowler*, ed. Craig R. Dykstra, Sharon Parks, and James W. Fowler (Birmingham, Ala.: Religious Education Press, 1986), 55.

12. Craig R. Dykstra, *Growing in the Life of Faith: Education and Christian Practices*, 2nd ed. (Louisville: Westminster John Knox, 2005), 159.

tion and the related engagements and appropriations of missional church theology that have been leading to the coalescence of a missional theology. While a consensus definition of missional theology remains elusive, I will present some of the foundational assumptions and inner dynamics of missional theology. I will show how missional theology is implicit in the functional missional church theology of George Hunsberger and the Gospel and Our Culture Network, and I will establish how it is explicit in the self-consciously academic missional theology of Darrell Guder, who is attempting to connect it to a history of theological development and define it as a discrete academic discipline.[13]

In chapter 3, I will develop the framework for understanding Craig Dykstra's theology of practices by introducing one strand of the contemporary practices discussion. By drawing on the greater body of work related to the Valparaiso Project and by paying special attention to the contributions of Dykstra and Dorothy Bass that generally frame the conversation, I will draw out some foundational assumptions that support their definition of Christian practices. I will introduce their succinct definition of a Christian practice and exposit that definition in terms of what I consider six crucial aspects of Christian practices, finally demonstrating how they all come to a focus in corporate worship.

In chapter 4, I will offer additional attention to Dykstra's writings on practices, ecclesiology, and educational ministry. There is evident in his writings on practices an openness toward and at times engagement with a missional perspective. It certainly would be possible to give his notion of practices a missional interpretation. His dynamic definition of faith, some of his statements explicitly connecting Christian education to mission, and some of his interaction with interlocutors whom I believe to be the progenitors of today's missional theology led me to believe this is the case. A series of phone interviews confirmed this missional impetus in Dykstra. His greater body of work, however, does not explicitly connect his reflection on Christian practices with what the missional theologian understands to be the nature and purpose of the church. This fact leads

13. Calling missional theology a "discrete academic discipline" is actually a little misleading. Guder's point is, as I will develop later, that the theological task is to be pursued in such a way that the entire understanding becomes missional. The term "missional" in "missional theology" provides temporary scaffolding that is used as long as the building needs it. When theology is done properly and is, in fact, missional, then the scaffolding term can be removed.

Claire Smith to conclude that mission is a "postscript" in Dykstra's work.[14] I am asserting his openness to having his own missional instincts advanced and having his notion of practices accented with the fundamental concerns of missional theology.

Out of the interaction with Dykstra, I will advance, in chapter 5, a constructive missional theological proposal about the possibilities and potential shape of missional Christian practices, adding to the broader discussion of Christian practices a missional interpretation that is founded on a clear statement of the mission and purpose of the congregation. I will not contrast Dykstra's notion of practices with a missional one or in any way diminish the great import of the practices way of thinking about faith and faith development. I will build on what Dykstra and the practices conversation have already contributed to the missional church discussion.

I will conclude with an epilogue that gives an example of how I have appropriated Dykstra's practices way of thinking about discipleship in my ministry with adolescents with special needs. I will also show how a missional theological perspective informs the way in which I comprehend and employ Christian practices.

14. Claire Annelise Smith, "Foundations for Missional Christian Education" (Ph.D. diss., Union Theological Seminary and Presbyterian School of Christian Education, 2005), 11-12.

CHAPTER TWO

The Missional Church
and Missional Theology

The word "missional" is becoming ubiquitous. But there is really no shared notion about what missional theology is — to this point there has been no substantive crosscurrent of conversation about the parameters and shape of missional theology. The purpose of this chapter is to introduce the reader to the streams of the discussion that make up my still-developing understanding of the concept of "missional theology" by giving a brief account of that conversation and the related engagements and appropriations of the theological interchange emerging from the missional church conversation.

As a starting point, my definition of missional theology follows: Missional theology is a kind of practical theology that explores in every aspect of the theological curriculum and praxis of the church the implications of the missionary nature of God with the purpose of forming congregations to better articulate the gospel and to live faithfully their vocation to participate in the ongoing redemptive mission of God in a particular context.

From its earliest expressions, missional theology has had at least three foundation stones. First, missional theology includes fundamental theological convictions regarding the missionary nature and initiative of God. Second, missional theology embodies a conviction, building on the insights of Lesslie Newbigin and the three-cornered relationship between the gospel, a church, and a particular culture, about how this missionary God calls the church to participate in his mission. Third, missional theology is a

way of thinking theologically that must animate every aspect of the theological curriculum and the congregation's life. Missional theology is not
another adjectival theology competing for a voice among other theologies.
In fact, the way missional theology is gaining shape and coherence is
through its interaction with a range of theological disciplines. I hope to
contribute to the development and coherence of missional theology by
placing it in dialogue with the contemporary practices conversation.

In this chapter I will introduce the reader to two of the primary expo-
nents of missional church theology, George Hunsberger and Darrell
Guder, and highlight their distinctive contributions. Finally, I will give an
example of how missional theology continues to develop as it draws energy from cross-disciplinary dialogue by offering the example of the
growing discussion about missional hermeneutics.

The Missional Theologies of
Darrell L. Guder and George R. Hunsberger

Two influential missional theologies in the missional church conversation
are those of Darrell L. Guder, Henry Winters Luce Professor of Missional
and Ecumenical Theology at Princeton Theological Seminary, and
George R. Hunsberger, professor of Missiology at Western Theological
Seminary. Guder's point of departure for considering a missional theology is the theological work of some antecedents whom he considers the
progenitors of the discipline. He gives significant attention to the curricu-
lar implications of the doctrine of *missio Dei* and to the theological justification for the missional church in the doctrine of God. His approach tends
to be more academic and curriculum-oriented than that of Hunsberger.
With respect to Christian practices, Guder emphasizes how the practices
will prepare the congregation for its commission to be a witness to the
kingdom of God.

Hunsberger's approach, while also thoroughly theological, is intentionally social scientific and addresses more deeply issues of culture and
context than does Guder's. Missional theology is not only to prepare future teaching elders or congregations for mission; missional theology is
the articulation of the gospel in a particular context. Hunsberger emphasizes a methodology or a missiological orientation that will guide the
church in negotiating the space between culture bashing and culture ab-

sorption. In other words, Hunsberger's work complements Guder's by providing a methodology to what Guder is asking missional theology to do across the theological curriculum and in congregations. With respect to practices, Hunsberger emphasizes how the practices as "living demonstrations" of the "ways of Christ" and as "patterns of missional faithfulness" are the embodiment of the congregation's witness. The following sections will expound their missional theologies.

The GOCN and George R. Hunsberger's Missional Church Theology

The Gospel and Our Culture Network (GOCN) in North America grew out of a parallel conversation in Great Britain initiated by the writings of Lesslie Newbigin about the relationship between the gospel and Western culture. The GOCN has attempted to carry forward in North America Newbigin's theological program of fostering a missionary encounter with the West, and George Hunsberger has been a leader of that movement.[1]

Early GOCN newsletters established a corpus of texts via bibliographies, quotes, and book reviews; acknowledged sympathetic seminars, symposiums, colloquiums, lectureships, programs, and conferences; and introduced a common language surrounding the discussion. In November 1989 a group of four (Wilbert Shenk, Craig Van Gelder, Charles West, and George Hunsberger) met at Princeton to determine the distinctives of the emerging network and settled on two. The network was to address missiological issues and had to be intentionally and self-consciously North American.[2] They determined that they would issue a personal invitation to key people interested in the network's purposes to attend lec-

---

1. "Bishop Lesslie Newbigin's recent writings have raised the issue of the Gospel's missionary encounter with Western culture in a way which has gripped many of us and sharpened our sensitivity to this most urgent contemporary calling. What *The Other Side of 1984* did for the churches of England, *Foolishness to the Greeks* has begun to do for us in the USA. Newbigin has directed what we have learned about Gospel and culture encounters elsewhere to the situation in our own culture." George R. Hunsberger, *Gospel and Our Culture* 1, no. 1 (December 1987): 1. Newbigin subsequently published another major book on those themes as he continued to wrestle with the issue of the unfinished agenda in his own Western culture: J. E. Lesslie Newbigin, *The Gospel in a Pluralist Society* (Grand Rapids: Eerdmans, 1989).

2. George R. Hunsberger, "Network News," *Gospel and Our Culture* 2, no. 1 (June 1990): 1.

tures by Newbigin at Western Theological Seminary in Holland, Michigan, in October 1990. These twenty people were also invited to remain for a day following the lectures in order to determine the questions and issues the emerging network needed to address.[3]

Special interest meetings for the GOCN were held at Lausanne II at Manila in 1989, and workshops were offered at the SCUPE[4] Congress on Urban Ministry in the spring of 1990. When in October 1990 George Hunsberger "mapped the terrain" in order to offer further direction to the network, he offered three distinctives: evangelizing North American people, relating to the social order, and giving focus to the church. Hunsberger commented, "New ways to put the questions, new frameworks for reckoning with them, and new proposals for configuring the church's *missional* life are beginning to surface."[5] This description of the church's life as intended to be "missional" represents the first instance of the term in the literature associated with GOCN and sets the stage for the ecclesiological agenda of the network. The agenda has to do with the very identity of the church in the midst of an acknowledged "third disestablishment" of the U.S. church, or, in other words, in the loss of place or the "fundamentally changed position of the church in our present society."[6] In line with the conclusion of the contemporary practices discussion, as we will see in a subsequent chapter, Hunsberger adds, "Such an ecclesiological agenda is served by the disciplines of Christian nurture and spiritual formation."[7]

3. *Gospel and Our Culture* 3, no. 1 (1991): 2.

4. Seminary Consortium for Urban Pastoral Education.

5. George R. Hunsberger, "Mapping the Terrain: A Proposal," *Gospel and Our Culture* 2, no. 2 (October 1990): 1, emphasis mine. Alan Roxburgh and M. Scott Boren have just published a handy book that gives a very brief summary of the missional church discussion. The authors lift up three themes that animate the discussion: the notion that the West is today a mission field, *missio Dei*, and Newbigin's vision of the church as a sign, instrument, and foretaste of the kingdom. The authors give a fine presentation of what "missional" is not, but do not offer a strong presentation of the theological conversation that has nurtured and shaped missional theology. They suggest that the word "missional" was introduced in 1998, and this is true only insofar as that was the year in which *Missional Church* was published. As I have made clear from reference to the GOCN newsletters, the word and developing conception of "missional" were operative already in 1990. For more on Roxburgh and Boren's take on missional theology, see Alan J. Roxburgh and M. Scott Boren, *Introducing the Missional Church: What It Is, Why It Matters, How to Become One* (Grand Rapids: Baker, 2009), 30-34.

6. Hunsberger, "Mapping the Terrain," 4.

7. Hunsberger, "Mapping the Terrain," 5.

By July 1991 a clear statement of the purpose of the GOCN was articulated:

> The Gospel and Our Culture Network exists for the purpose of encouraging the missionary encounter of the gospel with our North American culture. It is founded on a common commitment to give attention to the form of witness to Jesus Christ which is required in our present context. This purpose statement implies four critical orientations: a) that the encounter must be understood in terms of the dynamics of the interaction between the gospel and any particular culture, i.e., in "cross-cultural missionary perspective"; b) that the encounter must be based on a clear appreciation for the distinctive character of our contemporary North American culture (and cultures) as compared with other cultures and other forms of Western culture; c) that the encounter must have primary concern for the missionary identity of the local congregation in this particular cultural and historical setting; d) that the encounter must be by nature interdisciplinary and dialogic.[8]

As the newsletters and later books make clear, the discussion of gospel, culture, and church must be integrated and always related to the central task mentioned above: witness to Jesus Christ in the present context. Having established ecclesiology as a major theme of the GOCN discussion, the GOCN produced important monographs and essays on the issue in the following years. It is within this larger conversation about the identity, nature, and purpose of the church that the early definition and methodology of missional theology are embedded.[9] The methodology is illustrated in Hunsberger's Newbigin triad, an approach to negotiating the gospel-church-culture relationship founded on the theological insights of Lesslie Newbigin. This missional methodology helps a congregation avoid submission to culture in a way that the distinctiveness of its message is absorbed into culture and helps it escape an intransi-

8. George R. Hunsberger, "Major Consultation Readied," *Gospel and Our Culture* 3, no. 2 (July 1991): 1.

9. "[H]ow can the churches find their identity as alternative communities which live by loyalties and understandings different from the dominant culture or cultures? The life of the church as community, the sense in which the community casts and affirms an alternate 'world,' and the way the community learns to think of itself as representative of the reign of God are all implied." Hunsberger, "Major Consultation Readied," 5. These concerns also form the setting of the practices discussion in the GOCN.

gent sectarianism whereby the congregation never realizes its own reliance on culture or calling to impact its culture with the gospel. The Newbigin triad helps practical theologians to appreciate the dynamics that emerge around the axes of encounter: the "conversion-encounter" axis; the "reciprocal relationship" axis; and the "missionary encounter" axis.

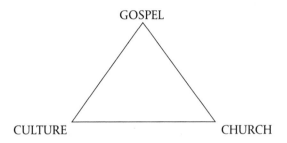

In Hunsberger's Newbigin triad,[10] the gospel-culture axis is the "conversion-encounter" axis. That is to say, the message must be translated into the thought forms and linguistic categories of a specific locale and must confront a culture with an embodied challenge. This embodied challenge reminds us that there is no such thing as a culture-free gospel and that the people of any culture who embrace the gospel must face a radical, though not total, discontinuity because the gospel both embraces and calls into question all cultures. The same Bible to which the church attempts to remain faithful in its presentation of the gospel continually challenges and reforms the particular expression of the gospel that the church articulates. It is along this axis that the insights of Lamin Sanneh are germane: the gospel theologically enfranchises the indigenous voice,[11] and this new perspective on the fullness of the gospel can challenge and be challenged by other expressions and articulations of the gospel. However, at the same time that the gospel liberates cultures, it is also a prisoner to culture because it is incarnated by a community that is conditioned by a

10. For a brief exposition of Hunsberger's Newbigin triad, see George R. Hunsberger, "The Newbigin Gauntlet: Developing a Domestic Missiology for North America," in *The Church between Gospel and Culture: The Emerging Mission in North America*, ed. George R. Hunsberger and Craig Van Gelder (Grand Rapids: Eerdmans, 1996), 3-25.

11. Lamin O. Sanneh, *Translating the Message: The Missionary Impact on Culture*, American Society of Missiology Series, no. 13 (Maryknoll, N.Y.: Orbis, 1989).

particular time and place.[12] Therefore, to approach the fullness of the gospel we must be aware of our own limitations with respect to our comprehension of the gospel and pursue the gospel in the fullness of its cultural plurality.

The gospel-church axis is the "reciprocal relationship" axis. The gospel cannot be understood by a particular congregation except though the lenses of a particular, culturally conditioned, and limited tradition. This tradition informs how the congregation reads the Scriptures and determines what questions they ask of the text. At the same time, the local congregation is constantly confronted and challenged by a gospel that is, in Guder's terms, "always before us."[13]

As a congregation participates in this hermeneutical process, the church is formed to become, as Newbigin has put it, "the hermeneutic of the Gospel."[14] This concept carries two primary meanings. First, the surrounding contextual environment reads the gospel (in an external sense) by viewing the church. The church becomes the authentication of the gospel to the degree that its life and message are congruent. Second, the church with its plausibility structures offers not only the external example of life in accordance with the gospel but also the lenses through which one can properly understand the gospel.

The church-culture axis is the "missionary encounter" axis. Authentic conversion, free from cultural apprenticeship or imperialism, brings about a new expression of the pluriform church. Along this church-culture axis the notion of the church universal receiving expression in the fullness of her cultural pluriformity is further considered. As the plethora of culturally distinct congregations share together in ecumenical fellowship, the gospel expands into its fullness. Ecumenical dialogue is necessary to make sure that no particular cultural expression of the gospel is either nullified or deified.

The interaction described above provides the working agenda of the Gospel and Our Culture Network[15] and represents the substance and

12. Andrew F. Walls, "The Gospel as Prisoner and Liberator of Culture," in *The Missionary Movement in Christian History: Studies in the Transmission of Faith* (Maryknoll, N.Y.: Orbis, 1996).

13. Darrell L. Guder, *The Incarnation and the Church's Witness*, Christian Mission and Modern Culture (Harrisburg, Pa.: Trinity, 1999), 148-49.

14. Newbigin, *The Gospel*, 222-33.

15. Hunsberger and Van Gelder, *The Church*, 2.

method of Hunsberger's missional theology. To see an example of Hunsberger's missional theology at work, see Thomas John Hastings's appropriation of his Newbigin triad to explicate his own experience of the tensions between gospel, church, and culture in Meiji, Japan, and to develop his own missional-ecumenical model of practical theology.[16] It could be argued that Hunsberger's approach to missional theology is simply a healthy practical theology. He merely employs the tools of a missiologist (anthropology, sociology, and theology) to perform Osmer's interpretive (Why is this going on?), normative (What should be going on?), and pragmatic (How might we respond?) tasks.

Darrell L. Guder's Contribution to "Missional Theology"

In agreement with Hunsberger, Guder characterizes the whole missional church discussion as having been, "at its core, a response to Lesslie Newbigin's question: Can the church in the West become, again, a missionary church, given the fact that its context has become a mission field?"[17] Guder's missional theology is a discipline that evolved out of this discussion, yet it has brought into the conversation some new emphases. The task of missional theology within this discourse, according to Guder, is to challenge the church to consider the consequences of the fact of its fundamental missionary nature for its structures, proclamation, offices, discipleship, and practices.[18] Guder's missional theology may be characterized, therefore, as a polemical theology, grounded in the rediscovery of the missionary nature of the triune God, that explores, in every aspect of the theological curriculum and in the discipleship of the church, the implications of the widely affirmed consensus that the church is missionary by its very nature.

Guder builds upon the work of those he interprets as forerunners of the field and adds his own nuance to the shape and role of the incipient missional theology. His conversation partners include, among others, the ecumenical statesmen John Mackay and Lesslie Newbigin as well as David Bosch and, particularly, Karl Barth. Guder, as a professor of missional and

16. Thomas John Hastings, *Practical Theology and the One Body of Christ: Toward a Missional-Ecumenical Model,* Studies in Practical Theology (Grand Rapids: Eerdmans, 2007).

17. Darrell L. Guder, "Worthy Living: Work and Witness from the Perspective of Missional Church Theology," *Word and World* 25, no. 4 (Fall 2005): 424.

18. Guder, "Worthy Living," 426.

ecumenical theology, is attempting to transform theological thinking by offering missional theology some definition and carving out a niche for it within the theological curriculum. Therefore, Guder gives more attention to distinguishing it from previous approaches to the study of mission and theology, defining missional theology and suggesting how it should function within the theological encyclopedia.

Background

To appreciate Guder's missional theology, it is necessary to understand how mission studies have developed over the past few decades. Early mission studies were a reflection of the great century (the nineteenth century) of missionary expansion,[19] which could aptly be described in caricature as a missionary movement without theology and apart from the church. Mission as "expansion" (i.e., the expansion of Western Christianity geographically, the expansion of Christianity by the increase of adherents, or the expansion of Western Christianity's influence), mission scholars would agree today, is not an adequate focal point for mission studies, yet it has been a dominant motif in how mission has been engaged and studied. The primary reason for this is that movements of Christian expansion, related to the movement of Western Christianity expanding across borders into the non-Western world, have been the setting in which the missionary impulse has been rediscovered. Therefore, **missiology**,[20] as an aca-

19. Kenneth Scott Latourette, *A History of the Expansion of Christianity*, 7 vols. (New York: Harper and Brothers, 1937), 4:7.

20. Perhaps the most referenced/called upon definition of missiology is that of Johannes Verkuyl: "Missiology is the study of the salvation activities of the Father, Son, and Holy Spirit throughout the world geared toward bringing the kingdom of God into existence. . . . Missiology's task in every age is to investigate scientifically and critically the presuppositions, motives, structures, methods, patterns of cooperation, and leadership which the churches bring to their mandate. In addition missiology must examine every other type of human activity which combats the various evils to see if it fits the criteria and goals of God's kingdom which has both already come and is yet coming." This comprehensive task includes a collaborative relationship with the theological disciplines of evangelism, biblical studies, hermeneutics, the branches of systematic theology, ethics, church history, the "science of religion," and the "nontheological" disciplines of cultural anthropology, sociology, economics, and political science, among others. Johannes Verkuyl, *Contemporary Missiology: An Introduction* (Grand Rapids: Eerdmans, 1978), 5. Missiologist Stanley Skreslet, who has made several recent contri-

demic discipline, developed in light of this process. The most significant
work of the early twentieth century was Gustav Warneck's text, the first
modern missiology text, *Evangelische Missionslehre*.[21]

Warneck's subtitle, "An Attempt at a Mission Theory," suggested that
he was proposing a theory of missions, and, in fact, in one of the volumes
he did attempt to secure a foundation for missions in terms of the truth of
Christendom, ethics, biblical theology, ecclesiastics, ethnology, and history. However, for the most part Warneck's missiology represented a
phenomenological and pragmatic engagement with the mission agencies
and organizations in an effort to aid missionaries in their attempt to come
to grips with their work in a complex and expansive mission field.[22]
Warneck's phenomenological and pragmatic approach to missiology
tended to keep mission and theology separated.[23]

The cleft between mission and theology was exacerbated by the distance between the missionary enterprise and the daily life of the churches
in the West. Lesslie Newbigin indicates that the most prolific period in
Protestant missions developed at a point in history when the churches
were "largely blind to the missionary implications of churchmanship." He
continues, "There was no other way in which those who were obedient to
the Great Commission could express their obedience except by forming
separate organizations for the purpose. It was thus that 'Missions' came to
mean something different from 'Church.'"[24]

---

butions to configuring the structure of mission studies, considers missiology a "nexus," "one
of the few places in the curriculum where primary studies of text, history, truth (i.e. systemat-
ics), and practice naturally intersect." Stanley H. Skreslet, "Nexus: The Place of Missiology in
the Theological Curriculum," *Association of Presbyterians in Cross-Cultural Mission Newsletter*,
no. 31 (April 1998). Elsewhere he states, "Missiology is not a recapitulation of the field of theology. Nor is it a new kind of social science or branch of history, although here, too, we find significant degrees of overlap due to the sharing of research methods and topics of mutual interest. The distinctive character of missiology is to be found rather in the way that it integrates
what appear to be contrasting concerns." Stanley H. Skreslet, "Configuring Missiology: Reading Classified Bibliographies as Disciplinary Maps," *Mission Studies* 23, no. 2 (2006): 198.

21. Gustav Warneck, *Evangelische Missionslehre: Ein Missionstheoretischer Versuch*, 3 vols.
(Gotha: F. A. Oerthes, 1897-1903).

22. See a summary of Warneck's *Evangelische Missionslehre* in Verkuyl, *Contemporary
Missiology*, 26-28.

23. Johannes Aagaard, "Some Main Trends in Modern Protestant Missiology," *Studia
Theologica* 19 (1965): 244.

24. J. E. Lesslie Newbigin, *One Body, One Gospel, One World: The Christian Mission Today*
(London: International Missionary Council, 1959), 25.

Since the Protestant missionary movement was animated by missionary societies, which had been organized and supported by laypersons and the so-called friends of mission, the modern missionary enterprise left the churches in the West largely undisturbed.[25] The result was, in Stephen Neill's words, "[A] failure of the Churches to develop a missionary sense that drove certain missionary societies to adopt positions and policies which were unrelated to anything in the New Testament, and then subsequently to attempt to work out a theological rationale for that which in itself is theologically indefensible."[26]

American missionary activity and the discipline of missiology advanced under these presuppositions about the relationship between missions, church, and theology, and traveled along the powerful currents of the supposed superiority of Western civilization, a sense of manifest destiny and responsibility that expanded the Puritan "errand into the wilderness" into an "errand to the world."[27] Eventually, with the success of the movement, the Americans would have to accept their status as *"goy b'goyim*, a people among peoples" in God's missionary plan.[28] However, in the nineteenth century the self-confidence of American missions and the belief that God's plan for the salvation of the world held a special place for North America were at an apex. Andrew Walls sums up the spirit of the American frontier missions movement with such phrases as: "vigorous expansionism; readiness of invention; a willingness to make the fullest

---

25. L. A. Hoedemaker, "The People of God and the Ends of the Earth," in *Missiology: An Ecumenical Introduction; Texts and Contexts of Global Christianity*, ed. F. J. Verstraelen (Grand Rapids: Eerdmans, 1995), 158.

26. Stephen Neill, *Creative Tension* (London: Edinburgh House Press, 1959), 84.

27. The title of William Hutchison's excellent work on American Protestant missionary thinking. William R. Hutchison, *Errand to the World: American Protestant Thought and Foreign Missions* (Chicago: University of Chicago Press, 1987). Hutchison promotes the thesis that it is possible to interpret the nineteenth-century missionary movement, "in its American expressions, as rooted both in a Christian, a-nationalistic zeal for expansion and active evangelization, and equally in a fervent belief, less obviously Christian but just as religious, that Americans were under special obligation to save and renovate the world" (8). Cf. Tomas Shivute, who observes, the "missionary expansion of the nineteenth century was influenced to a great extent by the contemporary mood of optimism and the conviction that foreign mission was a worthy means of bringing the light of the Gospel and the enlightenment of civilization to the entire world." Tomas Shivute, *The Theology of Mission and Evangelism in the International Missionary Council from Edinburgh to New Delhi* (Helsinki: Finnish Society for Missiology and Ecumenics, 1980), 187.

28. Hutchison, *Errand to the World*, 208.

use of contemporary technology; finance, organization and business methods; a mental separation of the spiritual and the political realms combined with a conviction of the superlative excellence, if not the universal relevance, of the historic constitution and values of the nation; and an approach to theology, evangelism, and church life in terms of addressing problems and finding solutions."[29]

The voluntary society, which marked American religion in general and the American dimension of the missionary movement in particular, was instrumental and pragmatic in nature, bringing together individuals, churches, and organizations in the interest of a common goal.[30] Due to the pragmatic function of the voluntary society, no theology of it was ever promoted.[31] The missionary movement was not sparked by reflective theologians who found in the self-revelation of God a missionary impetus. Missiology engaged a missionary movement instigated by people who, moved by the Holy Spirit, took initiative to proclaim the gospel to foreign lands.[32]

Not only were mission and church separated in practice, they were separated in theory and in the creeds and confessions of the churches. Since the missionary enterprise was only "churchly" in the sense that mission entails the establishment of churches in the non-Christian lands, in its early years the doctrine of the church played a less important role in

29. Andrew F. Walls, "The American Dimension of the Missionary Movement," in *The Missionary Movement in Christian History*, 234-35.

30. Andrew F. Walls, "Missionary Societies and the Fortunate Subversion of the Church," in *The Missionary Movement in Christian History*, 242. See also Mark Noll's use of Walls to make an interesting point about just how the American model of Christianity and voluntarism has had an appreciable impact on the way churches are organizing themselves around the world, in Mark A. Noll, *The New Shape of World Christianity: How American Experience Reflects Global Faith* (Downers Grove, Ill.: IVP Academic, 2009).

31. Walls, "Missionary Societies," 246. "There was never a theology of the voluntary society," explains Walls. "The voluntary society is one of God's theological jokes, whereby he makes tender mockery of his people when they take themselves too seriously. The men of high theological and ecclesiastical principle were often the enemies of the missionary movement."

32. "The missionary enterprise has not come into being through conscious theological reflection on the self-revelation of God in Christ, but through the descent upon certain men or certain groups of men — we cannot express it otherwise — of a compulsion of the Holy Spirit to undertake the proclamation of the Gospel overseas." Wilhelm Andersen, *Towards a Theology of Mission: A Study of the Encounter between the Missionary Enterprise and the Church and Its Theology* (London: SCM, 1955), 13.

understanding the missionary movement. Guder comments that the first time the theme of mission occurs in the Presbyterian Church (U.S.A.) book of confessions is in paragraph XXXV of the Westminster Confession, a paragraph that was not added until 1903![33] Furthermore, this paragraph, "Of the Gospel of the Love of God and Missions," is not in the section that addresses ecclesiology.[34]

As it related to missionary activity, the church of the nineteenth century served missions as an administrative hub or corporation for individuals and groups who took initiative in missions on behalf of the church. Therefore, the church never took the missionary movement into its self-understanding.

But by the time one important arm of the ecumenical movement, the International Missionary Council (IMC), convened at Tambaram in 1938, the whole world came to be accepted as the object of mission, and the line between the European or Western "Corpus Christianum" and the non-Christian world was beginning to dissolve. This was, of course, partially due to the success of the missionary movement up to that point and in part related to the secularization of the West.

After Tambaram the path to a theology of mission that was more cognizant of the church emerged: "For this mutual discovery of Church and mission is not only a landmark in the evolution of the missionary enterprise," explains Wilhelm Andersen, "it is also a sign of the progressive theological rediscovery by the missionary enterprise of its own nature which is full of promise for the future. Anyone who wishes to make theological affirmations about missions must speak also about the Church."[35] In reflect-

33. *Book of Confessions: Study Edition*, Part I of the Constitution of the Presbyterian Church (U.S.A.) (Louisville: Geneva Press, 1996), 214-15.

34. Darrell L. Guder, "The Nicene Marks in a Post-Christendom Church," in *Perspectives — an Online Publication of the OGA*, October 2006.

35. Andersen, *Towards a Theology*, 29. Hendrik Kraemer, in his preparatory work for the Tambaram conference, described this missionary nature of the church in terms of apostolicity. "The Church and all Christians, if they have ears to hear and eyes to see, are confronted with the question: What is its essential nature, and what is its obligation to the world?" He then answers, "The essential nature of the Church is that it is an *apostolic* body. It is this, not because its authority is derived from the apostles, for the apostles belong to the Church, but because in all its words and actions it ought to be a bearer of witness to God and His decisive creative and redeeming acts and purposes. To become conscious of its apostolic character is for the Church the surest way to take hold of its real essence and substance." At Tambaram the missionary enterprise was reoriented to the fact that it is inextricably related to the

ing on Tambaram, Karl Hartenstein summed up the missiological senti-
ment of the 1930s when he announced, "Whoever says mission, says
church," and "Whoever says the church, says mission."[36]

The publication of Wilhelm Andersen's *Toward a Theology of Mission* in
1955 and Gerald Anderson's *Theology of the Christian Mission* six years later
clearly marks the emergence of **theology of mission** as a discipline.[37]
Theology of mission, or mission theology, is concerned with, according to
Anderson, an early spokesman of the discipline, "the basic presuppositions and underlying principles which determine, from the standpoint of
Christian faith, the motives, message, methods, strategy and goals of the
Christian world mission . . . the source of mission is the Triune God who is
himself a missionary."[38] As a kind of loci-centered theology, theology of
mission replaced the pragmatic and programmatic "how to" questions of
the earlier missiology with questions about the nature, content, purpose,
and validity of Christian mission.

Missional Theology: Toward a Definition

Whereas theology of mission accompanied mission or attempted to justify mission, Guder's missional theology may be easily distinguished from
theology of mission in that with missional theology, explains Guder, "we
have arrived at the broadly affirmed consensus that the church is mission-

---

church's apostolicity. Hendrik Kraemer, *The Christian Message in a Non-Christian World*, 7th ed.
(Grand Rapids: Kregel, 1969), 1-2.

36. Karl Hartenstein, "Was haben wir von Tambaram zu lernen?" in *Das Wunder der
Kirche unter den Völkern der Erde: Bericht über die Weltmissions-Konferenz in Tambaram*, ed. Martin
Schlunk (Stuttgart: Evangelischer Missions-Verlag, 1939), 194. Tomas Shivute gives the following explanation: "Both Church and mission were seen as apostolic. . . . From this theological position there was no longer any justification in maintaining a mission organization
alongside a Church organism, since both were equally charged with the missionary obligation. In this connection the Church has, thus, discovered the essential missionary and theological nature of its being." Shivute, *The Theology of Mission*, 193-94.

37. Andersen, *Towards a Theology of Mission*, and Gerald H. Anderson, *The Theology of the
Christian Mission* (New York: McGraw-Hill, 1961), respectively. Missiologist Charles Van
Engen considers Anderson's work to be the first text of the discipline: Charles Edward Van
Engen, *Mission on the Way: Issues in Mission Theology* (Grand Rapids: Baker, 1996), 18.

38. Stephen Neill, Gerald H. Anderson, and John Goodwin, *Concise Dictionary of the
Christian World Mission*, World Christian Books (Nashville: Abingdon, 1971), 594.

ary by its very nature, and we are exploring the theological implications of that consensus."[39] This is the most succinct and most accurate representation of Guder's missional theology. What began with reflection on the church was challenged by the worldwide spread of the gospel through the missionary movement. That process challenged missions at the foundational level and shifted the emphasis in mission studies from talking about missions (human and church initiatives) to talking about mission (the mission of the triune God in which the church participates). "Missional" in the sense that Guder is employing the term relates to a larger theological discussion not only about missionary activity but also about the very nature of the church and, beyond that, about the nature of God as revealed through the gospel. Missional theology attempts to work methodologically in every aspect of the theological curriculum and the church's life in light of this fundamental recognition of the church's missional character. With respect to theology, this means "mission accompanies theology by asking questions about theology's motive, matter, and manner."[40]

The *motive* of missional theology is to prepare the congregation for their witness in the world. The *matter* of missional theology is that gauntlet of interaction in a specified locale among a congregation, a culture, and the gospel as well as a rereading of all the loci of theology from the perspective of the missional identity of the early Christian movement. The *manner* of missional theology relates to the way in which the community undertakes this theological task: Does the way in which a congregation practices missional theology contribute to the witness of that congregation?[41]

Guder began his Payton Lectures at Fuller Theological Seminary by explaining the concept of "missional" and exposing its intended polemical value according to those who recovered the term. The term was intended to capture and summarize the idea that the church is missionary by its very nature. Guder continues, "By adding the suffix 'al' to the word 'mission,' we hoped to foster an understanding of the church as fundamentally and comprehensively defined by its calling and sending, its purpose to serve God's healing purposes for all the world as God's witnessing people

39. Darrell L. Guder, "From Mission and Theology to Missional Theology," *Princeton Seminary Bulletin* 24, no. 1 (2003): 47.

40. Guder, "From Mission and Theology," 47.

41. Guder, "From Mission and Theology," 47-54.

to all the world."[42] The GOCN usage of the term "missional," asserts Guder, was an attempt to bring to the forefront the neglected notion that the church is by nature essentially missionary and, therefore, mission cannot be reduced to one of the many activities of the church.

In fact, the first place the phrase "missional theology" appeared in GOCN literature was in a GOCN newsletter in September 1993, where it was used to describe a distinct discipline that serves to nourish and inform the missionary identity of the church.[43] From the beginning, missional theology intended to "accompany and support the church in its witness by testing all that the church says and does in terms of its calling to be Christ's witnesses."[44]

Recent institutionalizations of missional theology have signaled its emergence and have contributed to further its shaping and coherence. At the forefront of this aspect of the missional theology conversation is Darrell Guder. Aside from the efforts of Guder and others at Princeton Theological Seminary to introduce a missional theological way of thinking into the curriculum, several other programs attempt to sustain education with a missional focus. At Biblical Seminary in 2008, John R. Franke was inaugurated the Lester and Kay Clemens Professor of Missional Theology. In this position he helps the seminary pursue its mission of preparing "missional leaders." Drawing on Barth, Newbigin, Bosch, and Guder, Professor John Franke offers the following mission-informed definition of theology: "Christian theology is an ongoing, second order, contextual discipline that engages in the task of critical and constructive reflection on the beliefs and practices of the Christian church for the purpose of assisting the community of Christ's followers in their missional vocation to live as the people of God in the particular social-historical context in which they are

---

42. Darrell L. Guder, "Walking Worthily: Missional Leadership after Christendom," Payton Lectures, May 2-3, 2007, Fuller Theological Seminary. *The Oxford English Dictionary* offers the following definition of "missional": "Relating to or connected with a religious mission; missionary." J. A. Simpson, E. S. C. Weiner, and Oxford University Press, *The Oxford English Dictionary*, 20 vols., 2nd ed. (New York: Clarendon, 1989). The dictionary offers as an early citation of the word a text from 1907, *The Age of Justinian and Theodora: A History of the Sixth Century A.D.* Interestingly, in that text the word is used adjectivally by the author to discuss the lament concerning how the patronage of Theodora supported the missionary efforts of the Monophysites! William Gordon Holmes, *The Age of Justinian and Theodora: A History of the Sixth Century A.D.*, vol. 2 (London: G. Bell and Sons, 1907), 687-88.

43. "Work Group Agendas (I)," *Gospel and Our Culture* 5, no. 3 (September 1993): 7.

44. Guder, "From Mission and Theology," 47.

situated."[45] Theology is by nature connected to the witness of the congregation. Therefore, theology must no longer be conceived of as having a mission component but should instead be understood as a "missional theology." As Franke explains, "What makes it particularly missional is its focus on the situated and provisional character of theology and its purpose in assisting the Christian community in its calling and vocation to participate in the mission of God."[46]

The missional theological approach is shared by Luther Seminary, Tyndale Seminary in Toronto, and Western Theological Seminary. Luther Seminary's Strategic Plan, *A Bold and Faithful Witness: Keeping the Promises of Our Mission,* lists "missional" among the three adjectives that describe and define their theological identity as a confessionally Lutheran and biblical seminary. The document reads, "Faithful responsiveness to the current context for the sake of proclamation is the evangelical impulse that informs our teaching and drives all reform. Toward this end, we commit ourselves to sensitive and thorough engagement with our contemporary settings and cultural contexts, to ongoing dialogue with partners from around the globe who can best teach us about the needs of the world, and to a willingness to assess and adapt our efforts in service to greater fidelity to the gospel of God."[47] The whole theological program serves the goal of producing graduates who will "lead Christian communities in apostolic mission for the sake of God's world."[48]

Tyndale Seminary in Toronto also takes seriously the missional calling of the church. As their literature affirms, "One of the distinctives of Tyndale Seminary is the framing of theological education in a missional understanding of the Church. We see theological education as 'formation for mission,' that is, the formation of leaders who participate in the mission of God in the world and who faithfully engage culture with the Gospel."[49]

45. John R. Franke, *Teaching Theology from a Missional Perspective,* available from http:www.biblical.edu/images/connect/PDFs/TeachingMissionalTheology.pdf (accessed August 23, 2007). What Franke acknowledged is described by Guder: "When we describe theology as missional, then we do imply that the work of theology is not an end in itself but is related to God's mission in the world." Guder, "From Mission and Theology," 49.

46. E-mail correspondence with John R. Franke, August 23, 2007.

47. *A Bold and Faithful Witness: Keeping the Promises of Our Mission,* at http://www.luthersem.edu/strategic_plan/pdfs/Strategic_Plan_05-05-08.pdf, 8 (accessed October 6, 2008).

48. *Bold and Faithful Witness,* 10.

49. http://www.tyndale.ca/seminary/about.php (accessed October 6, 2008).

Finally, Leanne Van Dyk describes how missional church principles have influenced the vocational identity of the individuals and the institution of Western Theological Seminary. According to Van Dyk, missional theology has influenced the curriculum, internal and external community life, and faculty research interests.[50]

While the institutional expressions of missional theology are recent, Guder understands himself to be carrying on a work that has been under way since the thirties.[51] He is continuing to ask how the Christendom project and its failure have impacted the self-understanding of the church, particularly as it relates to her primary calling. Guder finds forerunners of the field in theologians such as John Mackay, Lesslie Newbigin, David Bosch, and especially Karl Barth.

John Mackay contributed significantly to Guder's understanding of the post-Christendom church[52] and his conviction that the Western congregation is to be prepared for a missionary engagement with its own culture.[53] In agreement with Mackay, Guder recognizes that this task will

50. Leanne Van Dyk, "The Formation of Vocation — Institutional and Individual," in *The Scope of Our Art: The Vocation of the Theological Teacher*, ed. L. Gregory Jones and Stephanie Paulsell (Grand Rapids: Eerdmans, 2002).

51. "I am compelled by the desire to be a good steward of the already well developed and provocative process of missional theology that has coalesced in the last seven decades." Guder, "From Mission and Theology," 49.

52. John Mackay recognized that with the end of Christendom the formerly Christian lands had become a frontier. Accordingly, he concluded in the 1940s, the church must prepare itself to face the new frontier. In light of the new position of the post-Christendom church, Mackay affirmed that the unsettled and dislodged church must be prepared to be mobile, to live in "campaign tents" rather than "cathedrals." Most importantly, and presciently, Mackay added, "the Church must be made to realize that unless it is missionary it is simply not the Church. . . . The Church is the Church only when it is the missionary instrument of God's will." John Alexander Mackay, "With Christ to the Frontier," in *Renewal and Advance: Christian Witness in a Revolutionary World*, ed. Charles W. Ranson and International Missionary Council (London: Edinburgh House Press, 1948), 203.

53. In what has become a salient theme in Guder's missional theology, Mackay continued to express his understanding of the church in terms of this calling: "The Church's structure and doctrine, her liturgy and even her sacraments, fulfill their highest function, and express their deepest meaning, when they prepare the people of God to be the servants of God." John Alexander Mackay, "The Christian Mission at This Hour," in *The Ghana Assembly of the International Missionary Council, 28th December, 1957 to 8th January, 1958; Selected Papers, with an Essay on the Role of the I.M.C.*, ed. International Missionary Council and Ronald Kenneth Orchard (London: Edinburgh House Press, 1958), 121. See especially John Alexander Mackay, *Ecumenics: The Science of the Church Universal* (Englewood Cliffs, N.J.: Prentice-Hall, 1964).

necessitate new congregational structures and a new accompanying theology of mission.[54] He also, like Hunsberger, has been formed by Newbigin's missional ecclesiology and missionary engagement of a plural, post-Christendom Western culture. However, his most distinctive theological contribution to the discussion has arisen out of his interaction with the theological concept of *missio Dei* and the theological program of Karl Barth.

Missio Dei and Guder's Missional Theology

Mission scholar James Scherer makes an important observation that prior to 1950, the study of the "theology of mission" in today's sense of justifying the enterprise hardly existed: "The discipline was not considered necessary, and much good mission work was carried on without the benefit of serious theological reflection." Mission practice, methods, and phenomenology were considered, but "no fundamental consideration was given to the justification and necessity for mission work until that activity was called into question."[55] The era in which the Great Commission or the Student Volunteer Movement watchword[56] provided a self-evident missionary goal had passed.[57] The progressive encounter between mission,

54. Recognizing that the new frontiers of mission include the formerly "Christian" West, John Mackay wrote in *A Preface to Christian Theology*: "Christian theology today has a missionary role to fulfill of a kind that has not been required since the early Christian thinkers outthought the pagan world. Time was when both thought and action in secular society were basically determined by Christian conceptions. . . . But when things, taken for granted for centuries, are called in question, and total disintegration threatens, and secular theologies emerge, Christian theology is invested with a new missionary role." John Alexander Mackay, *A Preface to Christian Theology*, James Sprunt Lectures, 1940 (London: Nisbet and Co., 1942), 65. He would call for such a theology sixteen years later at the IMC conference at Ghana when he announced: "The time is clearly ripe to probe deeply into the theology of *mission*; it is no longer enough to raise questions regarding the policy of *missions*." Mackay, "The Christian Mission," 104.

55. James A. Scherer, *Gospel, Church, and Kingdom: Comparative Studies in World Mission Theology* (Minneapolis: Augsburg, 1987), 35-36.

56. "The evangelization of the world in this generation."

57. James A. Scherer, "Mission Theology," in *Toward the Twenty-First Century in Christian Mission: Essays in Honor of Gerald H. Anderson, Director, Overseas Ministries Study Center, New Haven, Connecticut, Editor, International Bulletin of Missionary Research*, ed. Gerald H. Anderson, James M. Phillips, and Robert T. Coote (Grand Rapids: Eerdmans, 1993), 195.

church, and theology since the World Missionary Conference in Edinburgh, 1910, the so-called "China shock" and the closing of China to missionaries due to the communist revolution, the progressive decoloniza-
tion of the emerging nations no longer under Western paternity, the
independence of India, impending war in Korea, and the crisis of a secularized Christendom had challenged the 150 years of mission thinking that
had assumed the legitimacy of the missionary enterprise. It was no longer
perceived as true that "the most testing days of the Christian mission, at
least for our generation, lay behind" but, rather, "the most testing days of
the Christian mission in our generation lie just ahead."[58] By the Willingen
conference of the IMC in 1952, the ecumenical movement had reached a
point at which the validity of the church's mission could be "treated as a
problem and not as an axiom."[59]

The IMC conference at Willingen, therefore, emphasized God's initiative, the missionary acts of God (what would later develop into *missio Dei*,
or mission of God theology), and the servant nature of the church's mission. If missions were to exist, they were to be God's responsibility and
they were to be "Missions under the Cross."[60] Such a cruciform approach
to missions reminds one at once of both the revelation and hiddenness of
God in Christ. From the standpoint of gauging the value and accomplish-
ments of missions, missions under the cross remind us that God's missionary presence does not depend on the success of the missionary enterprise. Therefore, outward appearances (e.g., numerical increase in
converts or any other visible markers of missionary success) cannot be the
standard by which missions are judged. Theologically, the cross keeps the
idea of the mission of God from being a timeless speculative truth — it is
because of God's intervention in Christ that one can even speak of the
missio Dei.

In response to these insights, mission studies appropriately moved
beyond the phenomenological methodologies that had dominated the

58. Norman Goodall, "Willingen — Milestone, Not Terminus," in *Missions under the
Cross: Addresses Delivered at the Enlarged Meeting of the Committee of the International Missionary
Council at Willingen, in Germany, 1952; With Statements Issued by the Meeting*, ed. Norman Goodall
(London: Edinburgh House Press; distributed in the U.S.A. by Friendship Press, New York,
1953), 11-12. The former quote is taken from the IMC conference at Whitby, 1947, and the later
from Willingen, 1952.

59. Andersen, *Towards a Theology*, 14.

60. The title of the conference report from Willingen: Goodall, *Missions under the Cross*.

early twentieth century to the point that, as Hoedemaker suggests, Willingen marked the end of "precritical and in a sense pretheological discourse on mission."[61] As Wilhelm Andersen would later state, "The basis and decisive recognition for a theology of missions consists in this: *Mission has its source in the Triune God*."[62]

While Willingen did "take the missionary movement back to the primary source of mission," Willingen did not capitalize on the new Trinitarian basis of mission by addressing the issue before it, and "the missionary movement lost its sense of direction."[63] This task would be left to the emerging *missio Dei* theology. The Willingen conference and the conversation about mission theology that it initiated became a touchstone for missional theology, as I will explain below.

David Bosch, in his masterful *Transforming Mission*, includes "Mission as *Missio Dei*" as one of the thirteen elements of his "Emerging Ecumenical Paradigm" of mission theology.[64] He notes a decisive shift in the past half-century away from understanding mission soteriologically (in terms of "saving souls"), culturally (in terms of extending the benefits of Western culture), or ecclesiocentrically (where the church is the initiator and the goal of mission). The emerging consensus has been to consider the mission in which the church participates in terms of God's mission. Bosch offers a definition of the classical doctrine of *missio Dei* wherein the "sending," in which God the Father sends the Son and the Father and the Son send the Spirit, is expanded to comprehend the Father, Son, and Spirit sending the church into the world. Within this paradigm, "mission is not primarily an activity of the church, but an attribute of God."[65] According to Bosch, one of the early promoters of this line of thinking was Karl Barth, whose insights can be found in his Brandenburg lecture, "Theology and Mission in Today's Situation."

In his Brandenburg lecture, which has become so important to Guder's missional theology, Barth made two important points about *missio Dei* theology, though he never used the term. First, only God, the

---

61. Hoedemaker, "The People of God," 164.

62. Wilhelm Andersen, "Further Toward a Theology of Mission," in *The Theology of Mission*, ed. Gerald Anderson (New York: McGraw-Hill, 1961), 301.

63. Shivute, *The Theology of Mission*, 199-200.

64. David Jacobus Bosch, *Transforming Mission: Paradigm Shifts in Theology of Mission*, American Society of Missiology Series, no. 16 (Maryknoll, N.Y.: Orbis, 1991), 389-93.

65. Bosch, *Transforming Mission*, 390.

God who sent the Son and the Spirit, can act to justify mission. Second, since mission does not belong to the church, the church's task is to point away from itself, yet its task is to point nonetheless. The church's missionary life is therefore eccentric, pointing away from itself to the source of its life, and not ecclesiocentric.[66]

According to Bosch, and what has become the received tradition, this thinking gained momentum and was framed by Hartenstein and received sinew and tissue at the IMC conference at Willingen, 1952.[67] After this approach to *missio Dei* was summarized and promoted by Georg Vicedom in his *Missio Dei* and *Mission of God: An Introduction to a Theology of Mission*, it was popularized and digested to become somewhat of a consensus in both "evangelical" and "ecumenical" circles.[68]

Bosch also sustained the notion promoted by H. H. Rosin and Jacques Matthey that there is a classical *missio Dei* doctrine that is faithful to the origins of the theology, and a modified or more radicalized *missio Dei* that emerged in the 1960s. The classical doctrine is understood to be the original intent of *missio Dei*, and it emphasizes the church's being brought into the sending activity of the triune God. The second *missio Dei* is seen to be a distortion of the first, represented by the Missionary Structure of the Congregation project of the WCC, in which God is active in secular history and political revolution and the church is to join in by pointing to signs of God's activity. Matthey, additionally, discerns a third trend in *missio Dei* theology, which is a balanced position comprehending both God's universal mission and the specific role of the church in that mission. This third trend offers "a clear formulation of the broader aspect of God's mission without neglecting to emphasize the role of the church in God's overall mission."[69]

66. Karl Barth, "Theology and Mission in the Present Situation" (lecture given at the Brandenburg Mission Conference, Berlin, April 11, 1932; unpublished translation by Darrell L. Guder).

67. Particularly through his contribution to Walter Freytag, ed., *Mission Zwischen Gestern Und Morgen* (Stuttgart: Evang. Missionsverlag, 1952).

68. For more on the origin of the *missio Dei* concept, see H. H. Rosin, *Missio Dei: An Examination of the Origin, Contents, and Function of the Term in Protestant Missiological Discussion* (Leiden: Inter-university Institute for Missiological and Ecumenical Research, 1972). One of the seminal texts of *missio Dei* theology is Georg F. Vicedom, *Missio Dei: Einführung in eine Theologie der Mission* (Munich: C. Kaiser, 1958); Georg F. Vicedom, *The Mission of God: An Introduction to a Theology of Mission* (St. Louis: Concordia, 1965).

69. Jacques Matthey, "Missiology in the World Council of Churches: Update; Presentation, History, Theological Background and Emphases of the Most Recent Mission State-

Importantly, as it relates to Bosch's impact on Guder's missional theology, Tiina Ahonen believes that it is possible to trace the roots of a comprehensive missional church theology in the works of Bosch grounded in this third, balanced *missio Dei*.[70] "In my own personal belief," argues Ahonen, "the comprehensive understanding of the missional church and the balanced position among *missio Dei* theologies are significantly indebted to David Bosch's missiological contributions."[71] Whether one accepts Matthey's distinction between a pristine, originally intended *missio Dei* and a later humanistic or secularized version, Ahonen certainly accurately presents some of the most important features of *missio Dei* theology and how they contribute to Bosch's, and subsequently Guder's, understanding of a missional church theology. Both Bosch and Guder uphold a Trinitarian intention of the *missio Dei* and avoid identifying God's mission with historical and sociological forces; they agree that God's mission is concerned with God's kingdom; they affirm that God is the author of mission — it does not issue from historical accident, church initiative, or human agency; and Bosch affirmed, in line with today's missional theology, that "it is not the church which 'undertakes' mission; it is the *missio Dei* which constitutes the church."[72] However *missio Dei* is understood, certainly these are among the most significant and agreed-upon contributions and are assumed dicta of Guder's missional theology.

Guder has articulated his understanding of *missio Dei* theology and how it relates to missional theology in "The Missio Dei: A Mission Theology after Christendom." Following Theo Sundermeier's scheme,[73] Guder

---

ment of the World Council of Churches," *International Review of Mission* 90, no. 359 (October 2001): 429-30.

70. Tiina Ahonen, "Antedating Missional Church: David Bosch's Views on the Missionary Nature of the Church and the Missionary Structure of the Congregation," *Swedish Missiological Themes* 92, no. 4 (2004): 586. Ahonen characterizes Bosch's contribution to mission theology as "comprehensive" because, in Bosch's mission theology, the origin of Christian mission lies not with the church only or in the world and historical movements "outside" the church. "The starting point is a double one. It is, at the same time, in the church and in the world, and, in the final analysis, it is beyond them both, in God. Therefore, missional self-understanding of the church should be based on both ecclesiological and contextual analyses, in the framework of the basic Trinitarian theology."

71. Ahonen, "Antedating Missional Church," 576.

72. Bosch, *Transforming Mission*, 519.

73. Theo Sundermeier, "Missio Dei Today: On the Identity of Christian Mission," *International Review of Mission* 92, no. 367 (2003): 560-78.

emphasizes that *missio Dei* theology offers important guidance for the post-Christendom church. It reminds the church of the mystery of God and the impossibility of defining or controlling divine revelation — Western theological traditions are not normative for the world. *Missio Dei* theology, therefore, emphasizes the importance of respecting the freedom and culturally distinctive responses of others and challenges notions of evangelism that are built upon coercive methods or theories of consumerism. It highlights the importance of cultural pluralism, boundary crossing, and edifying confrontation. Finally, *missio Dei* theology accents the importance of recognizing that mission takes place in space and time, which is, for the church, shaped by the reign of God. Guder concludes, "The *missio Dei* as expounded in terms of its mystery, freedom, pluralism, and thick hope, generates not one mission theology, but many — to equip the saints in all their cultural settings for the missionary vocation. *It is, in fact, a way of doing theology, better conveyed perhaps by the term 'missional theology.'*"[74]

Karl Barth and Guder's Missional Theology

Along with the doctrine of *missio Dei*, Karl Barth's theology has become increasingly important to Guder's conception and articulation of missional theology. A brief survey of how Barth lays the foundation for a missional understanding of God in the doctrine of election and how this implicates the missional church is crucial to comprehending Guder's missional theology.

The richest section of Barth's *Church Dogmatics* for constructing a missional theology is the section of his *Doctrine of Reconciliation* (book IV) entitled "The Task ['Commission' is a preferable translation to 'Task'] of the Community."[75] Barth begins by noting that the Christian community is not sent by God into the world "haphazardly or at random, but with a very definite task [commission]."[76] Barth elaborates the content of this

74. Darrell L. Guder, "The Missio Dei: A Mission Theology after Christendom," in *News of Boundless Riches: Interrogating, Comparing, and Reconstructing Mission in a Global Era*, ed. Lalsangkima Pachuau and Max L. Stackhouse (Delhi: ISPCK, 2007), 25, emphasis mine.

75. Karl Barth, *The Doctrine of Reconciliation*, vol. IV/3.2 of *Church Dogmatics*, ed. G. W. Bromiley and T. F. Torrance (Edinburgh: T. & T. Clark, 1962), 795-830.

76. Barth, *The Doctrine of Reconciliation*, 795.

commission, the content of this gospel that is given to the community. He explains that it is Jesus Christ who gives the community its commission and Jesus Christ who is, in fact, the content of the commission. "To use the simplest and biblical formulation," explains Barth, "'Ye shall be witnesses unto me.'"[77] The electing activity of God in Christ is the lens through which the various activities of the congregation, what Barth terms the living community of the living Lord Jesus Christ, must be understood.

"The election of grace is the whole of the Gospel, the Gospel *in nuce*,"[78] states Barth. That is to say, at its *nucleus* or at the kernel of the gospel is the doctrine of election, and this election by grace is the basis of our vocation.[79] We are elected with a trajectory. We are sent. For Barth, the doctrine of reconciliation (comprised of the doctrines of justification, sanctification, and vocation) is merely the logical expression and expansion of his doctrine of election as articulated in his doctrine of God.[80] In Barth's estimation, the doctrine of election has nothing to do with an eternal decree — "some sort of darkness beside, behind, or above the revealed God."[81] There is no "*decretum absolutum*. There is no will of God different from the will of Jesus Christ."[82] Barth is arguing against formulations of the doctrine of election in which a deeper ground for God's action is found in God's eternal decree than in God's self-revelation in Christ and that place God's sovereign freedom to act in an immovable dogma outside of and beyond God's action in Christ. Instead, argues Barth, God reveals himself as the electing God in the concrete act of election that has already and actually taken place. As Otto Weber suggests, Barth sets the doctrine of election "in motion."[83] In the name "Jesus Christ" the electing God and the elected man coincide.[84] In becoming Jesus Christ, God reveals his solidarity with human-

77. Barth, *The Doctrine of Reconciliation*, 796-97.

78. Karl Barth, *The Doctrine of God*, vol. II/2 of *Church Dogmatics*, ed. G. W. Bromiley and T. F. Torrance (Edinburgh: T. & T. Clark, 1957), 13-14.

79. Barth, *The Doctrine of Reconciliation*, 484.

80. Bruce McCormack confirms this interpretation in Bruce McCormack, "Grace and Being: The Role of God's Gracious Election in Karl Barth's Theological Ontology," in *The Cambridge Companion to Karl Barth*, ed. John Webster (Cambridge: Cambridge University Press, 2000).

81. Otto Weber, *Karl Barth's "Church Dogmatics": An Introductory Report on Volumes 1:1 to 3:4*, trans. Arthur C. Cochrane (Philadelphia: Westminster, 1953), 94.

82. Barth, *The Doctrine of God*, 124.

83. Weber, *Karl Barth's "Church Dogmatics,"* 93.

84. Barth, *The Doctrine of God*, 63.

ity in that, at once, "Jesus Christ is the electing God" and "Jesus Christ is the elected man."[85] Rather than a *decretum absolutum*, Barth formulates a *decretum concretum* — an electing in Christ from the very beginning.[86]

After explaining that God in Christ elected himself for fellowship with humanity, Barth next turns to the community, the living congregation. At this point he draws out the implications of the doctrine of election for the missional church. The congregation is "that human fellowship which provisionally forms in a special way the natural and historical environment of the man Jesus."[87] As a human fellowship, its special character is its witness that corresponds to the prophetic role of Jesus Christ. The apostolicity of the community, the fact that the community is a fellowship under obligation to the world, is generated from the fact of God's election of himself for fellowship with humanity in Christ and God's election of all people in Jesus Christ. "It is because this is so, because the call comes to it from the man whom God has elected and loved," argues Barth, "that the community of Jesus Christ and the men united in it are bound to the world and everywhere summoned to action in relation to it. For God's active intervention for man, *His eternal election of all men in the One*, His giving of this One for all, His Word which goes out to all in this One, is the basis of its own being and existence."[88] Founding the commission of the community on election in Christ allows for an authentic solidarity between the Christian community and the world that is, from Barth's perspective, very natural yet has proved terribly elusive in many works on the mission and ministry of the church.

Barth is in complete agreement with the ecumenical conversation on this point that the Protestant ecclesiologies of his time, inherited from the sixteenth and seventeenth century, have no goal beyond the church herself, and the benefits, temporal and eternal, of her members.[89] This aspect of inwardness, this failure to address the meaning and purpose of the Christian community, is what Barth deems the "yawning gap" in ecclesiology.[90]

85. Barth, *The Doctrine of God*, 111 and 124, respectively.
86. Weber, *Karl Barth's "Church Dogmatics,"* 95. For a concise summary of Barth's doctrine of election, see Eberhard Busch, *The Great Passion: An Introduction to Karl Barth's Theology* (Grand Rapids: Eerdmans, 2004), especially 106-27.
87. Barth, *The Doctrine of God*, 216.
88. Barth, *The Doctrine of Reconciliation*, 777.
89. Barth, *The Doctrine of Reconciliation*, 766.
90. Barth, *The Doctrine of Reconciliation*, 766.

The deeper issue that allows for such a misunderstanding of the ecclesial practices is a misdirected conception of vocation, one that begins in the Christendom paradigm with infant baptism and introduces vocation later as a special phenomenon. Barth argues that to be a Christendom Christian, no vocation is required at all. Christianity is "naturally passed on with his mother's milk and the water of baptism."[91] Barth is raising serious objections to the notion that vocation should be linked with Christian status and challenges the prevailing belief that election is something less than an essential aspect of Christian existence.[92] He concludes that "the goal of vocation is not a special Christian existence but the existence of the Christian as such, and that the existence of the Christian is either grounded in his vocation or not at all."[93]

Barth develops the critique further when addressing the issue of the *beneficia Christi* in the section subtitled "Christian as Witness."[94] The problem with the classical understanding of the individual Christian's vocation is that it is simply a reflection of the church that exists for itself. This inward church defines a Christian not by his or her apostolic movement, following and impelled by Christ into the world, but, instead, "it is the fact that they are and have and may do these things specifically which makes them Christians and thus constitutes the distinctive feature or principle of Christian existence and the essential goal of vocation."[95] This attenuated and reduced definition of a Christian in no way resembles the God who called him or her into being.[96] It completely misses the fact that the essence of vocation is that God makes the man or woman into his witness. The task, or rather the commission, to which Christians are called and in which they exist consists in the fact that "with their whole being, action, inaction and conduct, and by word and speech, they have to make a definite declaration to other men."[97] The union with Christ that Barth expounds as the goal of vocation is a union of working with Christ and not a static union. It is a fellowship of apostolic action. Barth defines the Christian not as the possessor of the

91. Barth, *The Doctrine of Reconciliation*, 523.
92. Barth, *The Doctrine of Reconciliation*, 522.
93. Barth, *The Doctrine of Reconciliation*, 524.
94. Barth, *The Doctrine of Reconciliation*, 545-614.
95. Barth, *The Doctrine of Reconciliation*, 562.
96. See the discussion of reductionism in Darrell L. Guder, *The Continuing Conversion of the Church*, Gospel and Our Culture Series (Grand Rapids: Eerdmans, 2000), 120-41.
97. Barth, *The Doctrine of Reconciliation*, 575.

beneficia Christi but as witness. The church is not the institute of salvation that distributes the *beneficia Christi* but the living community of the Lord Jesus Christ and his provisional representation in the world. "We are thus given a fuller and sharper understanding still of the *nota ecclesiae* visible in this context," explains Barth. "The true community of Jesus Christ does not rest in itself. It does not merely contemplate the striving of the world with its better knowledge. It does not refrain from active participation. It [the church] exists as it actively reaches beyond itself into the world."[98] The doctrine of election, which has often been the theological foundation of a vapid inwardness and has led to monikers like "the frozen chosen" for the Presbyterian church, has become for Barth an important element in the theological formulation of the missional congregation.

John Flett presents Barth's potential contribution to the concept of *missio Dei* in his dissertation "God Is a Missionary God: Missio Dei, Karl Barth, and the Doctrine of the Trinity." This is especially important because Guder's engagement of Barth's theology and his interaction with Flett over the past seven years as his adviser and colleague have had an appreciable impact on his theological perspective.

The thrust of Flett's dissertation is that *missio Dei* theology developed as a critical concept to distance the concept of mission from the contingent and troubled expressions of mission evident in the colonial missionary enterprise.[99] While *missio Dei* provided some theological relief and justification for mission by grounding mission in the Trinity, the doctrine of the Trinity provided no constructive direction for the concept.

How are Barth's theology and *missio Dei* theology really connected? Despite claims to the contrary by almost all thoughtful mission scholars, argues Flett, *missio Dei* theology as it has developed does not have its basis in the theology of Karl Barth. Flett intends, therefore, to reengage the *missio Dei* discussion by allowing Barth the impact that has been attributed to him without adequate foundation in the past half-century. To do that he presents Barth's theology as fundamentally missionary and demonstrates how Barth grounds his notion of mission in his doctrine of the Trinity. The doctrine of the Trinity properly understood does not allow the separation of God's act and being. Flett, following Barth, establishes on the rev-

98. Barth, *The Doctrine of Reconciliation*, 779.
99. John Graeme Flett, "God Is a Missionary God: Missio Dei, Karl Barth, and the Doctrine of the Trinity" (Ph.D. diss., Princeton Theological Seminary, 2007).

elation of the triune God in Christ the doctrine of the church that lives as it appropriately corresponds to the ongoing prophetic function of Christ. Therefore, the apostolic life of the community is not a second movement that is optional.[100] *Missionary participation is the form of human activity that corresponds to Christ's completion of his act, and it is the concrete form of human and divine fellowship, that is, union with Christ.* This observation is at the heart of missional theology.

Summary: Missional Theology, So Far

While I have highlighted some of the differences in approach and emphasis between Guder's and Hunsberger's missional theologies, they both agree that the church is chosen for something beyond itself and this fact is fundamental to its being. God's sending action, God's election, constitutes the church. In service of the *missio Dei*, Hunsberger's missional methodology of the Newbigin triad and emphasis on the cultural pluriformity of the gospel functions synergistically with Guder's emphasis on the theological formulation of the missional congregation, the *missio Dei*, and his commitment to drawing out the implications of the missional church thesis for academy and congregation. Given our earlier discussion of practical theology, one could argue that missional theology is a kind of practical theology.

So, again, my provisional definition of missional theology based on this discussion is: *Missional theology is a kind of practical theology that explores in every aspect of the theological curriculum and praxis of the church the implications of the missionary nature of God with the purpose of forming congregations to better articulate the gospel and to live faithfully their vocation to participate in the ongoing redemptive mission of God in a particular context.*

---

100. Hoedemaker suggests, "That the church is sent means that the inner dynamic of being a church and the world-relatedness of the church coincide. That is to say at the very minimum that it is impossible to view 'mission' as one of the many activities of the church grounded along with other activities in a comprehensive ecclesiology defined apart from the church's world-relatedness. It is equally impossible to regard the church as a secondary datum by comparison with the ongoing movement of mission and evangelization. For the process of conversion, which the missionary vision of the ends of the earth evokes from within the covenant between God and his people, constitutes the very content of what it is to be the church." Hoedemaker, "The People of God," 171.

The Continuing Conversion of Missional Theology

While some may seek something more definitive than the provisional definitions of missional theology offered so far, it is important to remember that missional theology is still an emerging discipline and a continuing conversation that finds new fuel and clarity of expression by engaging other disciplines. For example, in the past decade missional theology has developed in interaction with biblical studies in the progressive formation of missional hermeneutics. "It is impossible to read the New Testament," explains Bosch, "without taking into account that most of it was consciously written within a missionary context."[101] With these words, Bosch succinctly conveys one of the important foundations of missional hermeneutics, an approach to biblical interpretation that James Brownson, Michael Barram, and others have since developed.

Missional hermeneutics begins with the question, "What would it mean, and what might it look like to read the Bible self-consciously and with an explicit methodological starting point in an ecclesial location that is construed as fundamentally missional in cast and character?"[102] For the past seven years at the AAR and SBL conferences, Tyndale Seminary, Toronto, and the GOCN have sponsored a special session to consider this question. Why a missional hermeneutic? Because, answers Brownson, the early Christian movement that canonized the Scripture had a missionary character and because all interpretation must navigate the dialectic between our common humanity and common Scripture and the diversity of our cultural particularity. A missional hermeneutic recognizes that God is present, through his self-revelation in Scripture, in our accurate though provisional apprehensions across diverse cultural boundaries. The interpretive matrix of the gospel, explains Brownson, that served to proclaim information and "bring about a new state of affairs"[103] was the interpretive matrix that served the New Testament writers. Today the story of the life, death, and resurrection of Jesus Christ is still the center that brings co-

---

101. Bosch, *Transforming Mission*, 489.

102. "A History of the Conversation — Mission and Biblical Interpretation: Toward a Missional Hermeneutic," at http://www.gocn.org (accessed September 23, 2008).

103. James V. Brownson, "Speaking the Truth in Love: Elements of a Missional Hermeneutic," in *The Church between Gospel and Culture*, 254. For more on Brownson's approach, see James V. Brownson, *Speaking the Truth in Love: New Testament Resources for a Missional Hermeneutic*, Christian Mission and Modern Culture (Harrisburg, Pa.: Trinity, 1998).

herence to our various interpretations of Scripture. As Christianity crosses cultural boundaries, as we affirm the plurality of interpretations of Scripture, and as we remain committed to ecumenical dialogue and seek coherence and commonality, we are all brought together as we read our stories in the light of Christ.

Building on Brownson, Barram explains that a missional hermeneutic is "an approach to biblical texts that privileges the missiological 'location' of the Christian community in the world as a hermeneutical key."[104] He continues, "The recent shift toward viewing the Bible as missiological in character offers a corrective to a reductionistic emphasis on a few putative 'mission' texts. Many are beginning to recognize that the church's mission hangs not on a few scattered passages, but on a much broader appeal to the activity of God as revealed in scripture as a whole."[105] In this way, missional theology has interacted with biblical studies. In fact, at Princeton Theological Seminary, Professors Darrell Guder (missional and ecumenical theology) and Ross Wagner (New Testament) have offered several courses in missional hermeneutics, including "1 Peter: Missional Hermeneutics and the Formation of the Church."[106]

It is the various guiding principles in missional hermeneutics that betray the contours of the functional missional theologies behind them. For example, Christopher Wright and Michael Goheen suggest that the biblical theme of the mission of God, which is the thread woven throughout the warp and woof of the Scriptures, is the hermeneutical key for all engagement of Scripture. As I have noted above, Guder and Wagner submit that there has always been a missional intent in the Christian Scriptures — the documents were intended to equip God's people to participate in his ongoing redemptive mission. Barram suggests that missional theology should help us to understand the point of reference from which we are ad-

104. Michael Barram, "The Bible, Mission, and Social Location: Toward a Missional Hermeneutic," *Interpretation* 61 (2007): 42-43.

105. Barram, "Bible, Mission," 44.

106. Offered at Princeton Theological Seminary in the spring semester, 2008, as NT 448/TH 448. The course description on the syllabus reads: "A cross-disciplinary investigation of the scriptural formation of the missional congregation as exemplified in 1 Peter. Working with exegetical and theological methods, we shall examine the contextualization of the Gospel in first century Asia Minor, asking how this letter shapes the community for witness. The implications of this investigation for our understanding of biblical authority and interpretation, for ecclesiology, and for exegetical discipline will be explored."

dressed by Scripture and should inform the kinds of questions that arise when we read Scripture. Finally, Brownson and Hunsberger apply insights from the gospel-church-culture interaction of the Newbigin triad to the hermeneutical process as they discern "the fundamental way the tradition and the context are brought into interaction, and the way that the 'gospel' then functions as a guide to the process."[107]

Following this example of the missional reorientation of biblical scholarship, I intend to bring the contemporary practices discussion into dialogue with missional theology. The next chapter will introduce the *Practicing Our Faith* conversation.

---

107. These various approaches, representative of the approaches to missional hermeneutics espoused and promoted at AAR, SBL, and through a variety of publications, are summarized in the following unpublished working paper: George R. Hunsberger, "Starting Points, Trajectories, and Outcomes in Proposals for a Missional Hermeneutic: Mapping the Conversation" (2008).

CHAPTER THREE

The Practices in the
Practicing Our Faith *Conversation*

In the previous chapter, I uncovered the foundation of today's missional theology in the work of the Gospel and Our Culture Network (GOCN), and, in particular, I noted Hunsberger's and Guder's contributions to the emerging discipline. From the standpoint of Hunsberger's missional theology I argued that it is essential to consider the three-cornered relationship between gospel, church, and culture and to consider the cultural pluriformity of the church. From the standpoint of Guder, I argued that it is crucial to explore the theological implications of the fact that the church is fundamentally defined in terms of her mission: her being gathered and upbuilt always have in view her being sent. I made the point that missional theology is an incomplete discipline and methodology that requires the fuel of conversation with other disciplines in order to develop.

I mentioned in chapter 1 the importance of the practices discussion for my ministry with adolescents with special needs. Therefore, this chapter will summarize that practices discussion in its own terms in order to set up that conversation. The Valparaiso Project's practices discussion, which has found expression in the *Practicing Our Faith* series, represents an enlivening trend in the field of practical theology. I believe their discussion of Christian practices is an important conversation partner that can contribute to the vitality of missional theology and can benefit from the missional church perspective. An examination of the *Practicing Our Faith* discussion will set the stage for considering more closely Craig Dykstra's theology of Christian practices.

Background for a New Approach to Practical Theology

The decline of mainline Protestantism has been the topic of many studies, books, and journal articles in the past two decades, and it has been the impetus for the renaissance and recasting of practical theology as a theological discipline in North America. The decline of mainstream denominations has been attributed to a lack of attention to traditional teaching, murky answers to important theological questions, and a related inability to foster commitment among parishioners;[1] the rise of a more educated society combined with a pluralistic religious atmosphere and rampant individualism;[2] an eschewing of gospel orthodoxy in a short-lived run for cultural relevance;[3] the fundamental loss of theological identity and vision and a disconnection from formative Christian practices resulting in an inability to nurture faith;[4] and a general diminished importance of religious denominations after World War II related to the increased role of government in American life that made the contribution of mainline churches unnecessary once they had forfeited that "spiritual" element to their social service that made them unique and vital.[5] There have even been amusing demographic explanations of mainline decline suggesting that higher fertility rates and better retention rates among more conservative churches have caused those churches to increase, unlike the reciprocal trend in their mainline Protestant counterparts.[6] No matter what the ebbing has been attributed to, most authors agree that the so-called mainline decline has occurred,[7] and many connect that trend in some way to the fact that the syn-

1. Dean M. Kelley, *Why Conservative Churches Are Growing: A Study in Sociology of Religion* (New York: Harper and Row, 1972).

2. Wade Clark Roof and William McKinney, *American Mainline Religion: Its Changing Shape and Future* (New Brunswick, N.J.: Rutgers University Press, 1987).

3. Thomas C. Reeves, *The Empty Church: The Suicide of Liberal Christianity* (New York: Free Press, 1996).

4. Milton J. Coalter, John M. Mulder, and Louis B. Weeks, *The Re-forming Tradition: Presbyterians and Mainstream Protestantism*, Presbyterian Presence (Louisville: Westminster John Knox, 1992).

5. Robert Wuthnow, *The Restructuring of American Religion: Society and Faith Since World War II*, Studies in Church and State (Princeton: Princeton University Press, 1988).

6. Michael Hout, Andrew M. Greely, and Melissa J. Wilde, "Birth Dearth: Demographics of Mainline Decline," *Christian Century* 122, no. 20 (October 2005).

7. Even historians like Diana Butler Bass who now believe that mainline churches are in a postdecline period of reorganization and revitalization do not deny the significant loss

thesis between religion and culture in America is in its twilight. In short, many of these studies represent a church discharged of its chaplaincy of society and attempting to come to grips with the end of Christendom.

The post-Christendom church, having been divested of ecclesiastical totalitarianism and sent to the sidelines in public discourse, is suddenly faced with the fact that it has been and is being, in the words of Diana Butler Bass, disestablished and "de-traditioned."[8] According to Dorothy Bass, the church has entered a postmodern and post-Christendom phase of life during which "many Christian people seem unaware of the rich insights and strong help the Christian tradition can bring to today's concerns"[9] because these inherited traditions have not necessarily provided meaning and direction in everyday life.[9]

In the words of theologian Douglas John Hall, the church in North America is undergoing a metamorphosis, a radical change in posture in American culture from Christendom to diaspora.[10] Having never attained legal establishment in our part of North America, Christianity found what has proven to be a more enduring way to become entrenched in American society — cultural establishment. As Hall puts it, "Christian establishment in North America has functioned more nebulously to undergird our official values, hopes, and moralities — what we like to call our way of life."[11] Today the situation has changed dramatically so that "most of the old, mainline denominations that once formed the backbone of the Christian establishment on this continent now find themselves depleted and increasingly, almost arrogantly, ignored by the centers of power."[12] Nonetheless, despite its anemic structures, the mind-set of North American forms of Christendom has proven resilient.

Contributing to the disestablishment of a North American form of

---

of status and prestige among mainline churches in America. Diana Butler Bass, *The Practicing Congregation: Imagining a New Old Church* (Herndon, Va.: Alban Institute, 2004), 9-11.

8. Diana Butler Bass, *The Practicing Congregation*, 21-33.

9. Dorothy C. Bass, ed., *Practicing Our Faith: A Way of Life for a Searching People* (San Francisco: Jossey-Bass, 1997), 5.

10. Douglas John Hall, "Metamorphosis: From Christendom to Diaspora," in *Confident Witness — Changing World: Rediscovering the Gospel in North America,* ed. Craig Van Gelder (Grand Rapids: Eerdmans, 1999). See also the third installment of his trilogy, Douglas John Hall, *Confessing the Faith: Christian Theology in a North American Context* (Minneapolis: Fortress, 1996), 201-64.

11. Hall, "Metamorphosis," 71.

12. Hall, "Metamorphosis," 71.

Christendom has been a narrative of rapid social change, whether in its enduring secularization form or with postmodern sensibilities. In this disorienting social climate the church is faced with some difficult questions. How are the shared ways of life in our communities changing, and where does the church fit in? How do we, as a church, engage a world that has been fragmented into disparate spheres, each sphere with its own interests, goals, and legitimating authority navigated by autonomous individuals? How does the church address the issue of pluralism in which the Christian religion becomes one system among other equal systems, including other religious systems? How does the Christian church sustain its identity in a culture that has disintegrated and when authority has become multivocal? Is it true now, along the lines of Robert Wuthnow's *After Heaven*,[13] that Americans have been seekers seeking a "life giving way of life," exploring spirituality due to some disaffection with the fast-paced and fragmented patterns of life in the modern world?

In summary, the conversation about Christian practices has arisen in a climate in which the "dominant culture" is rife with individualism,[14] is experiencing an unprecedented time of change, is infatuated with that which is novel and new, and is confused and misled by an aggressive market about what people fundamentally need.[15] For the mainline church it is a transitional time when it is necessary to ponder its changing role under such conditions. As Dorothy Bass has posed the issue, it is a time to consider how to make Sunday special when it is no longer protected by either customs or legislation.[16]

---

13. Robert Wuthnow, *After Heaven: Spirituality in America Since the 1950s* (Berkeley: University of California Press, 1998). Wuthnow participated in a Practicing Christian Faith conference with Dykstra and Bass in 1997 and presented the lecture "Contemporary American Spirituality." Whereas Wuthnow suggests that Americans have been seekers, his book promotes the idea, important to this discussion, that now Americans may be shifting from a seeker-oriented spirituality to a practice-centered spirituality. Dorothy C. Bass, Craig R. Dykstra, and Robert Wuthnow, "Practicing Christian Faith" (conference sponsored by the Louisville Institute for the Study of Protestantism and American Culture presented at Louisville Presbyterian Theological Seminary, Louisville, September 25-26, 1997).

14. Robert N. Bellah et al., *Habits of the Heart: Individualism and Commitment in American Life* (New York: Harper and Row, 1986).

15. Dorothy C. Bass, "What Is a Christian Practice?" September 2006; available from http://www.practicingourfaith.org/cfm/library/view.cfm?id=420&page=1&author=1 (accessed May 22, 2007).

16. Dorothy C. Bass, *Practicing Our Faith*, 83-84.

The coalescence of what has today become an important discussion in Christian education and practical theology about Christian practices can be discerned on the pages of *Initiatives in Religion,* the newsletter of the Lilly Endowment. The attempt to distinguish a Christian way of life that can be lived with integrity in a postmodern and post-Christendom North American setting was expressed in a call for a "full-blown, constructive practical/pastoral theology for the contemporary American church."[17] A possible solution was proposed in the subsequent issue of *Initiatives in Religion* when the project that resulted in *Practicing Our Faith* was introduced. The shared practices explored in that work, argued Dykstra, "may provide an important clue to how we might draw on ancient wisdom to 'choose life' in ways appropriate to our own time and circumstances."[18]

In addition to the reflection on Christian practices offered in the *Practicing Our Faith* series, which continues to develop under the auspices of the Valparaiso Project, several of Dykstra's essays were drawn together to become an important touchstone in the conversation. The essays contained in *Growing in the Life of Faith* span nearly three decades and are united in that they have informed a theological movement that is invested in the quality and depth of the practice of faithful Christian living.[19] As Dorothy Bass explains in the foreword to the second edition, the essays converge in that they address the "ongoing patterns of shared life in and through which Christian people experience and help one another to receive God's real, but still mysterious grace." Bass, whom Dykstra considers his closest colleague in developing the practices approach to Christian education in the faith and whom he credits as the one who saw in the occasional essays a coherent book, recognizes *Practicing Our Faith* and *Growing in the Life of Faith* as "starting points for a conversation on the life of Christian faith that continues today."[20] As

17. Craig R. Dykstra, "A Way of Life," *Initiatives in Religion: A Newsletter of the Lilly Endowment, Inc.* 5, no. 4 (Autumn 1996): 2.

18. Craig R. Dykstra, "Shared Practices," *Initiatives in Religion: A Newsletter of the Lilly Endowment, Inc.* 6, no. 2 (Spring 1997): 2.

19. Craig R. Dykstra, *Growing in the Life of Faith: Education and Christian Practices,* 2nd ed. (Louisville: Westminster John Knox, 2005), ix. "Dorothy's remarks tell the story of the place of this book in the theological movement of which it is a part. I am glad for that, because I have always seen my book to be part of that conversation even though much of it was written quite some time before 'Christian practices' became a prominent theme in theological education and church life."

20. In Dykstra, *Growing in the Life,* xxv and xv.

the church responds to the challenges of a new position in the world, so must the theological discipline that reflects on and guides her in her ministry in that world: practical theology.

New Directions in Practical Theology

One scholar who has recently mapped the terrain of and envisioned a new direction for practical theology in this new world is Kathleen Cahalan.[21] Cahalan offers a helpful survey of the practical theological landscape. According to Cahalan, many Christian educators and practical theologians in the past two decades have responded to Edward Farley's critique that the discipline of practical theology, (mis)understood as an "applied discipline," has been unevenly invested in the preparation of professional, ordained ministers to help them to sustain established congregations. This "clerical paradigm" has failed the ministers and the church in the face of disestablishment and secularization.[22] Cahalan suggests that the post-

---

21. Kathleen A. Cahalan, "Three Approaches to Practical Theology, Theological Education and the Church's Ministry," *International Journal of Practical Theology* 9 (2005). Also, see her article in Dorothy C. Bass and Craig Dykstra, eds., *For Life Abundant: Practical Theology, Theological Education, and Christian Ministry* (Grand Rapids: Eerdmans, 2008).

22. Farley's challenge to theological education to move beyond the clerical paradigm heavily impacted Craig Dykstra and finds resonance in the discussion surrounding missional theology. For example, Guder, coming from the angle of missional ecclesiology, trumpets the same concerns in his Payton Lectures: "The implications of the shift to missional ecclesiology are as daunting for theological education as they are for the practice of particular congregations. If we are educating for the inward-oriented sense of the church, then our graduates should be equipped to deal competently with the religious needs of the churches' members and to maintain the structures and traditions of the institutions that exist to address those needs. We continue to need ecclesiologies that focus on the attainment and preservation of the individualistic assurance of personal savedness, upon rites and sacraments, polities and ordered ministries, provision of services and programs to the religious consumer, and preservation of religious customs and celebrations valued by our secularizing culture. If, with Lesslie Newbigin, we are challenged to recognize that our own context has become, within an astonishingly short period of time, a post-Christian mission field, posing enormous challenges to the received forms and attitudes of western Christendom, then that inward-oriented, church-maintaining approach to theological education will not work. Education for maintenance is not the same thing as education for mission." Darrell L. Guder, "Walking Worthily: Missional Leadership after Christendom" (Payton Lectures, May 2-3, 2007, Fuller Theological Seminary). It is this underlying concern about the nature and purpose of the church and her educational ministry that makes Dykstra,

Christendom, postmodern setting of the North American church has spawned three primary approaches to practical theology, each casting its own vision for the ministry of the church in a post-Christendom setting. She characterizes these approaches, along the lines of Paul Lakeland's *Postmodernity: Christian Identity in a Fragmented Age,* as late modern, countermodern, and radical postmodern. Each model has in common three characteristics: "each approach has a particular reading of the post-modern situation based on an analysis of the Enlightenment's impact on Christian thought and practice . . . offers constructive proposals to advance the Christian community's attempt to live faithfully in secular post-Christendom . . . advances a model of the church's ministry with corresponding proposals for theological education."[23]

The late modern, for whom she offers the example of Don Browning, attempts to secure the foundation for ethics and ministry in a universal principle. In this sense, late moderns continue in some form the project of modernity whereby an objective science finds a basis for morals in a universal law. The radical postmodern, represented in Cahalan's article by feminist Rebecca Chopp, has embraced the fragmentation that is attendant to postmodernity and has eschewed the notion of a universal theological narrative, especially one that is Caucasian, middle-class, Western, and male dominated. It is, however, to the third approach to post-Christendom, postmodern practical theology, that we now turn our attention: that which Cahalan characterizes as the "neo-conservative/post-liberal variant of countermodernity" and is represented, to some extent, by the approach of Dorothy Bass and Craig Dykstra.[24]

Cahalan characterizes the countermodern approach to practical theology as one that, motivated and directed by Alasdair MacIntyre's *After Virtue,* embraces an Aristotelian virtue ethic and attempts "to retrieve values abandoned by the Enlightenment, either through metaphysics or the values and practices of a particular religious and cultural tradition."[25] Dykstra and Bass's practice-centered approach to practical theology represents one of the dominant efforts to renew the field.[26] What follows is an

whose ecclesiology is heavily influenced by Farley, and the missional theologian such compatible conversation partners.

23. Cahalan, "Three Approaches," 67.
24. Cahalan, "Three Approaches," 66.
25. Cahalan, "Three Approaches," 66.
26. Bass and Dykstra, *For Life Abundant.*

attempt to express their notion of Christian practices as it has been represented through the Valparaiso Project on the Education and Formation of People in the Faith and in the series of books related to it and stemming from *Practicing Our Faith.*

The Practices Discussion

By drawing on the greater body of work related to the Valparaiso Project and by paying special attention to the contributions of Dorothy Bass and Craig Dykstra that generally frame the conversation, I will, first, draw out some foundational assumptions that support their definition of Christian practices. Then I will state their succinct definition of a Christian practice and exposit that definition with what I consider to be six crucial aspects of Christian practices according to the *Practicing Our Faith* discussion, finally demonstrating how they all come to a focus in corporate worship. Last, I will indicate how the discussion's notion of Christian practices functions practically and concretely by considering Serene Jones's essay "Graced Practices: Excellence and Freedom in the Christian Life."

Foundational Assumptions

The Valparaiso Project's discussion of Christian practices is directed by several guiding assumptions. First, the study assumes that God is active and present in the world and is continuing God's work of reconciliation. This belief is foremost and foundational, and to miss this supposition is to risk allowing the practices discussion to deteriorate into another exploration of human action and social dynamics. While sociological and psychosocial studies are important to consider in theological reflection, this project is approaching the subject of practices from a confessional standpoint. Its understanding of Christian practices "presumes that Christian practices are set in a world created and sustained by a just and merciful God, who is now in the midst of reconciling this world through Christ."[27]

---

27. Craig Dykstra and Dorothy C. Bass, "A Theological Understanding of Christian Practices," in *Practicing Theology: Beliefs and Practices in Christian Life,* ed. Miroslav Volf and Dorothy C. Bass (Grand Rapids: Eerdmans, 2002), 21.

Second, and related, the Valparaiso Project represents an attempt to approach a way of life from the perspective of the human condition theologically understood. In other words, *Practicing Our Faith* betrays an implicit theological anthropology. In contrast to the many "needs" constructed in and marketed to our culture, the practices in this discussion address human needs that arise from fundamental human conditions to which every culture must respond if human life is going to flourish. Among these basic human conditions are finitude; the need for healing; the human need for community; the fact that humans are creatures of time who are vulnerable, encounter strangers, and need rest; and the fact that humans are sinful and in need of forgiveness. Christian practices are Christian because they acknowledge and address those needs with a theological understanding of finitude and a theological interpretation of how God calls us to live with one another under these conditions and in light of God's active presence in the world. To connect the first and second points, the redemptively transformative action of God, whereby God offers us hospitality, provides our model and the impetus for our response of hospitality to one another. Hospitality fulfills a need that all people have because, as humans, we are all vulnerable to isolation and alienation; at one time or another we are the stranger.

Third and finally, Bass, Dykstra, and their associates believe that large-scale communal ways of being in the world, what have been termed "practices," are foundational to how all communities are embodied and extended. Below I will explain this further, but for now it is sufficient to note that practices should not be confused with specific, discrete acts. Christian practices involve a constellation of acts, but as practices they are about a way of life — what Dykstra calls discipleship.[28] Such practices can be recovered from the Christian tradition, and these practices can help people to negotiate these disintegrating times and support human flourishing. These Christian practices are not about controlling or mastering the above-mentioned human conditions or about attempting to manipulate God and grace; instead, they "cultivate openness and responsiveness to others, to the created world, and to God."[29] As we will see, engagement

---

28. The term "discipleship" was not featured prominently in the Valparaiso discussion until the recent publication of *For Life Abundant: Practical Theology, Theological Education, and Christian Ministry*. The term is defined in Dykstra's work, and in a way that is appealing to the missional theologian. I will explore Dykstra's potential contribution to a sustained conversation with missional theology about Christian practices in the next chapter.

29. Dorothy C. Bass, "What Is a Christian Practice?"

in the practices is transformative or converting in such a way that participation in the practices offers direction for a faithful Christian life that is attuned to the present activity of God, informed by ancient wisdom of the Christian tradition, and oriented to the hopeful future.

These foundational assumptions help guide the discussion's understanding of what a practice is. Still, one more significant influence, mentioned above, deserves attention — the use of Alasdair MacIntyre's *After Virtue* to frame a definition of practice. Early on Dykstra found MacIntyre's presentation and definition of social practices to be helpful in overcoming the individualistic, technological, ahistorical, and abstract understanding of practice that he felt hampered theological education.[30] MacIntyre's well-known definition of social practices reads as follows: "By a 'practice' I am going to mean any coherent and complex form of socially established cooperative human activity through which goods internal to that form of activity are realized in the course of trying to achieve those standards of excellence which are appropriate to and partially definitive of, that form of activity, with the result that human powers to achieve excellence, and human conceptions of the ends of goods involved, are systematically extended."[31] According to Dykstra, practical theology and theological education as a whole have conformed to a culturally and socially prevalent understanding of practice such that practices, even understood as strategic and patterned actions, are primarily considered things that individuals do to effect certain outcomes via causal relationships outside of larger historical and moral considerations. In this view, practice is applied to a situation by means of historically neutral and abstract principles and methods in a technical fashion. MacIntyre helps Dykstra to articulate a paradigm shift in how practice is perceived in theological education and to introduce practices as historically elongated, communal ways of responding to fundamental human conditions.

Bass also found in MacIntyre a suitable pathway into the practices discussion. MacIntyre's category of "living tradition" as an argument that is "historically extended and socially embodied"[32] provided for Bass a way to

---

30. Craig R. Dykstra, "Reconceiving Practice," in *Shifting Boundaries: Contextual Approaches to the Structure of Theological Education*, ed. Barbara G. Wheeler and Edward Farley (Louisville: Westminster John Knox, 1991), 35. I will cover this article in depth in the following chapter.

31. Alasdair C. MacIntyre, *After Virtue: A Study in Moral Theory*, 2nd ed. (Notre Dame, Ind.: University of Notre Dame Press, 1984), 187.

32. MacIntyre, *After Virtue*, 207.

speak of American congregations as the fundamental bearers of religious living tradition and a paradigm for engaging the shared patterns of life and continuing corporate activities that are cardinal to and constitutive of those communities.[33]

However, to identify their approach to practices too closely with that of Alasdair MacIntyre is a mistake. As both Don Richter and Jonathan Wilson have pointed out, the main flaw with MacIntyre is that his theory necessitates yet does not offer either a specific, normative moral tradition as the foundation for his account of virtues, practices, and "the good life," or any specific practices.[34] MacIntyre is attempting to recover some form of the Aristotelian moral tradition; however, throughout his *After Virtue* no specific moral tradition is discernible.[35] The contributors to *Practicing Our Faith* and *Practicing Theology* are clear about the moral tradition that is foundational to their work: "The chapters are united by the authors' shared belief that practices find their deepest expression *in the activities of God.*"[36] They are calling upon the Christian tradition.

Unfortunately, when MacIntyre's concepts are employed, along with the benefits of receiving a conceptual framework for speaking about practices, a whole language is inherited from the social ethicist that often deflects the conversation from what it should be about: discipleship and the witness of the Christian community.[37] Too much ink can be invested in

33. Dorothy C. Bass, "The Education and Formation of People in the Faith" (Caldwell Lectures presented at Louisville Presbyterian Theological Seminary, Louisville, March 6-7, 1995).

34. Don Carl Richter, "Christian Nurture in Congregations: Ecclesial Practices as Social Means of Grace" (Ph.D. diss., Princeton Theological Seminary, 1992), 201.

35. Jonathan R. Wilson, *Living Faithfully in a Fragmented World: Lessons for the Church from MacIntyre's "After Virtue,"* Christian Mission and Modern Culture (Harrisburg, Pa.: Trinity, 1997), 54-57.

36. Dorothy C. Bass, *Practicing Our Faith,* 11, emphasis mine.

37. For an example of someone who critically engages and enhances MacIntyre's definition of social practices by reimagining them as ecclesial practices, see Richter, "Christian Nurture in Congregations." Richter discerns five significant features of MacIntyre's definition of social practices (they are communal, historical, experiential, dynamic, and cognitive) and then attempts to modify MacIntyre's definition by extending it using Edward Farley's phenomenological and theological analysis. For another who employs yet is cognizant of the limitations of MacIntyre's definition of a practice, see Wilson, *Living Faithfully in a Fragmented World.* More recently and concisely from Wilson, see Jonathan R. Wilson, *Why Church Matters: Worship, Ministry, and Mission in Practice* (Grand Rapids: Brazos, 2006), 9-23. Bryan Stone summarizes and critically appropriates MacIntyre's conception of practices in

explaining MacIntyre's concepts, converting them from the Aristotelian moral tradition to a more biblical moral tradition and connecting them to a contemporary discussion of practices. Aristotle's notion of *telos* is not an adequate substitute for the biblical notion of eschatology, which "antici-pate(s) the ultimate triumph of the kingdom of Jesus Christ, when all things will be subject to him,"[38] and suggests that this reign and rule have already been inaugurated in Christmas.

I do not believe that the *Practicing Our Faith* discussion has fallen into this trap. Nonetheless, one must ask what compromises, if any, have been made theologically by investing so heavily in MacIntyre's definition of practices. As Sarah Coakley has convincingly laid bare, MacIntyre's oft-quoted definition of a practice from *After Virtue* is about socially estab-lished *human* activity and *human* projects.[39] Furthermore, as Richter notes, the practices of the church, particularly what he terms the ecclesial prac-tices of proclamation, sacrament, and care, carry within them a "mission-ary impulse [that] requires the extension of these goods beyond social boundaries."[40] In some instances it appears as if human flourishing is the goal of the practices and that developing virtues and experiencing per-sonal spiritual growth are the ends.[41] The effort to engage a post-Christendom culture loses some powerful language of the faith in favor of ill-defined and unanchored terminology like "faithful," "authentic," "in-tegrity," "human flourishing," "what is true and good," which is united by the desire to "walk aright." As I will develop later, missional theology chal-lenges a revolution in theological orientation; it can help to define what constitutes a "good" and "faithful" practice by connecting the practices to the nature and purpose of the community that practices them.

Nonetheless, while the school of thought has drawn conceptually

---

his attempt to make the case for evangelism as a practice, in Bryan P. Stone, *Evangelism after Christendom: The Theology and Practice of Christian Witness* (Grand Rapids: Brazos, 2007).

38. Donald K. McKim, "Eschatology, Collective," in *Westminster Dictionary of Theological Terms* (Louisville: Westminster John Knox, 1996), 92.

39. Sarah Coakley, "Deepening Practices: Perspectives from Ascetical and Mystical Theology," in *Practicing Theology*, 80.

40. "As noted above, proclamation, sacrament and care are not only for the sake of the ecclesial community but are also for the sake of all the environments and life-worlds in which human beings exist. Another way of saying this is to say that all ecclesial activities have a non-provincial, self-surpassing, element that cannot be confined geographically or demographically." Richter, "Christian Nurture in Congregations," 271.

41. Dorothy C. Bass, preface in *Practicing Our Faith*, xiii.

from MacIntyre's articulation of practices as presented in *After Virtue*, it is not legitimate to consider this approach neo-Aristotelian along the lines of MacIntyre's project. On several occasions the authors have attempted to distance their notion of practices from that offered by MacIntyre.[42] In fact, while the influence of MacIntyre on the conversation cannot be denied, the conception of practices that Bass and Dykstra offer was, the authors claim, "entirely inductive," relying on the active discipleship of parishioners for its shape. The authors engaged concrete practices, reflected on embodied theology, and then formulated a definition with the aid of some of MacIntyre's concepts.[43] If Christian practices cannot be equated with MacIntyre's social practices, then what, according to this discussion, are "Christian practices"?

A Definition of "Christian Practices"

The Valparaiso Project, *Practicing Our Faith,* and the writings of its contributing authors are replete with definitions of "practice." Perhaps the most concise definition of a Christian practice is found near the beginning of *Practicing Our Faith* and again in *Practicing Theology*: "Christian practices are things Christian people do together over time in response to and in the light of God's active presence for the life of the world [in Jesus Christ]."[44] Conferences, mono-

---

42. For example, Dykstra writes, "In order to discern the significance of practice for Christian life, we have needed to move beyond MacIntyre's historical-moral claim to make epistemological-theological suggestions." Dykstra, "Reconceiving Practice," 47. Also, in the footnotes of "Christian Practices and Congregational Education in the Faith" there is an effort to deliberately distance their understanding of practices from that of Alasdair MacIntyre. The point is made that their conception of practices is *"loosely based* on the work of the moral philosopher Alasdair MacIntyre." Dorothy C. Bass and Craig R. Dykstra, "Christian Practices and Congregational Education in Faith," in *Changing Churches: The Local Church and the Structures of Change,* ed. Michael Warren (Portland, Oreg.: Pastoral Press, 2000), 262 n. 1, emphasis added. Their approach "differs in crucial ways from MacIntyre" in that it is "theological and thus normed not only internally but also through the responsive relationship of Christian practices to God." Dykstra and Bass, "A Theological Understanding," 21 n. 8.

43. Bass, Dykstra, and Wuthnow, "Practicing Christian Faith."

44. Dorothy C. Bass, *Practicing Our Faith,* 5, emphasis in original. The authors suggest in a footnote in *Practicing Theology* that the parenthetical words, "in Jesus Christ," absent from the original *Practicing Our Faith* definition, "would clarify the character and content of the active divine presence that is so central to our understanding of practices." Dykstra and Bass, "A Theological Understanding," 18 n. 3.

graphs, articles, and Web sites have been devoted to refining and exposing this definition and reflecting on its multifarious expressions in concrete forms.[45]

Six Aspects of Christian Practices

What follows is an attempt to discern the most important aspects of practices as they appear in the literature associated with the Valparaiso Project and the *Practicing Our Faith* and *Practicing Theology* projects. I suggest that in their perspective Christian practices have a historical aspect, a social aspect, a universal aspect, a local aspect, a conversional/transformational aspect, and a witnessing aspect. After expositing the definition of Christian practices in terms of these different aspects, I will describe how, in the Valparaiso literature, these practices come to focus in worship.

The practices of the Christian faith are *"things people do together over time"* and have a **historical** aspect. Christian practices come to us from the past and will be shaped by Christian communities for the future, or, as Dykstra has explained, the practices allow us to be inventive in the present, in the light of the past, and for the sake of the future.[46] This social history of Christian practices in various living traditions and cultures contributes to the larger understanding of any given practice. Therefore, practices cannot be severed from their past because the practices carry that history within themselves. As Dykstra notes, "the past is embedded in the practice itself. To abstract the practice from its tradition is to reduce the practice to a group activity."[47] Practices come into being through the process of social interaction over a sustained period of time. "As people participate in practices, they are involved in their ongoing history and may in the process significantly reshape them," explains Dykstra. "Practices may be deepened, enriched, extended, and to various extents be re-

---

45. Much of Dykstra's contribution to the Valparaiso discussion can be found in a compilation of his essays and occasional writings: Dykstra, *Growing in the Life of Faith*. More attention will be given specifically to Dykstra and his approach to Christian practices in the subsequent chapter. Among the more helpful resources is the explanation of Christian practices on the *Practicing Our Faith* Web site: http://www.practicingourfaith.org/prct_what_are_practices.html.

46. Bass, Dykstra, and Wuthnow, "Practicing Christian Faith."

47. Dykstra, "Reconceiving Practice," 44.

formed and transformed."[48] The fact that practices are irreducibly connected to a history does not mean, however, that they are static. The living members of the community of faith alter the tradition and leave their mark on the practices. As Bass has emphasized, Christian practices are part of a tradition, the Christian tradition, which is an ongoing argument about what exactly the shared patterns of our lives and the things in which we desire to participate are all about.[49]

Furthermore, if a Christian practice is historical, then it is not abstract. Principles, guidelines, techniques, and methods may not be abstracted from the history of the Christian tradition and used in a technical fashion to address a particular issue, solve a dilemma, or obtain a desired result.[50] Such an understanding of practices co-opts, deforms, reduces them to mere procedures or methods to engage present circumstances and misses the values and benefit of the practice qua practice. Practices as strategic and patterned actions, carried out by professional agents to create change in other persons using social scientific theories outside of larger moral considerations, are not what Bass and Dykstra are promoting. When this happens the practices are dislodged from the history out of which they develop, and their own internal momentum and living tradition, that which make them distinctive as Christian "practices," are abandoned.

The practices of the Christian faith are *"things people do together"* and have a **social** aspect. The social character of practices is primary — a tradition cannot be extended into the future or persist in the present apart from social forms of embodiment. That does not mean, obviously, that we do not engage in Christian practices as individuals; but it does mean that Christian practices are not individualistic. The practices are shared patterns of life that must be learned from others and done with others. Even a practice that is often engaged in alone, like prayer, is learned from others and connects one to a tradition and community of prayer. Furthermore, since the spiritual life is not individualistic, individual creativity is contributed to the community practice.

The practices of the Christian faith address *"the life of the world"* and therefore have a **universal** or fundamental aspect. Christian practices ad-

48. Dykstra, "Reconceiving Practice," 44.
49. Dorothy C. Bass, "The Education and Formation of People in the Faith."
50. Dykstra, "Reconceiving Practice," 38-41.

dress fundamental human needs and conditions, theologically understood, that are experienced across nations and span generations. As I will
explain below, it is possible for Christian practices to be completely
contextualized and local and at the same time move beyond parochialism.
The practices that Dykstra, Bass, and their associates have in mind are
large-scale communal responses to fundamental human conditions in
light of God's activity in Christ. Missionary scholar Andrew Walls has insisted in his missionary reading of diversity and coherence in historic
Christianity that there are convictions that are fundamental to all historic
expression of Christianity across the centuries.[51] In the same vein, the
Practicing Our Faith conversation seems to suggest that the Christian practices, by addressing fundamental or universal human needs, also bear
transnational family resemblances.

The practices of the Christian faith have a **local** aspect. Another way
to say this is that they have a contextual aspect such that each expression
of a practice is culturally shaped and in a provisional form yet authentically incarnated; practices are flexible enough to take on the texture and
contours of specific cultures and social settings. According to Bass and
Dykstra, "Christian practices appear in slightly different forms in each
unique local congregation and surrounding community."[52] These practices, while maintaining a family resemblance to Christian practices
worldwide, are textured by the fact that they are done at our church, in our
neighborhood, and in our workplaces across the various spheres of our
living.

The practices of the Christian faith are things Christians do *"in response
to and in the light of God's active presence"* and have a **transformational/
conversional** aspect. The practices that Dykstra and Bass have in mind
are not necessarily what one might consider ecclesial practices like baptism and the Lord's Supper; in fact, these practices are not addressed adequately in their works. Instead, Dykstra and Bass have in mind practices

51. Andrew F. Walls, "Culture and Coherence in Christian History," in *The Missionary
Movement in Christian History: Studies in the Transmission of Faith* (Maryknoll, N.Y.: Orbis, 1996),
23-24. Walls notes that there are certain "signposts" or "family resemblances" in historic
Christianity. He lists the worship of the God of Israel; the ultimate significance of Jesus of
Nazareth; the belief that God is active where believers are; the belief that believers constitute a people of God transcending time and space; and these people are marked by a common set of scriptures and the special use of bread, wine, and water.

52. Bass and Dykstra, "Christian Practices," 260.

that are constituted by the mundane activities of everyday life. These ordinary activities are "recruited," reoriented, and transformed in response to God's active presence in the world.[53] In this sense the practices are understood to be "arenas" that "put us where life in Christ may be made known, recognized, experienced, and participated in."[54] They are the means of grace by which the presence of God is palpably experienced and our doubts, fears, and suspicion that there are no realities behind the language and liturgies of the Christian faith are quelled: "In the midst of engagement in these practices, a community comes to such an immediate experience of the grace and mercy and power of God that the 'nasty suspicion' . . . simply loses its power."[55] So through these large-scale ways of being in the world, communities and individuals are transformed and reoriented in response to God's active presence in the world.

The claim that one puts oneself in a position to receive a certain kind of knowledge of God by participating in these historic Christian practices, Dykstra adds, is not the type that can be proven; it is the kind of claim for which one offers testimony or witness. More than social reinforcement, Christian practices are a means of grace, a place where one finds union with Christ and a participation in the practices of God: "After a time, the primary point about the practices is no longer that they are something we do. Instead, *they become arenas* in which something is done to us, in us, and through us that we could not of ourselves do, that is beyond what we do."[56]

---

53. Dorothy C. Bass, *Practicing Our Faith*, 5, 8-9.

54. Dykstra, *Growing in the Life*, 43.

55. Dykstra, *Growing in the Life*, 53. The "nasty suspicion" refers to Farley's claim that many fear that there is no more to religion than the religious broker. Farley is addressing the "practical atheism" that pervades the theological community. In his words, "In recent years the theological community has entertained what might be called a nasty suspicion about itself. The rumor did not arise within that community but, once implanted, it had a certain self-fulfilling effect. Could it be that there are no realities at all behind the language of this historical faith? Could it be that the testimony, the storytelling, the liturgical expressions of this faith refer to entities that have only phenomenal status? Could it be that the mode of human existence which this historical religion calls faith involves no cognizing, no apprehendings, at all? Are Christian theologians like stockbrokers who distribute stock certificates on a nonexistent corporation?" Edward Farley, *Ecclesial Man: A Social Phenomenology of Faith and Reality* (Philadelphia: Fortress, 1975), 6.

56. Dykstra, *Growing in the Life*, 56. And again: "I have been arguing that the practices of the life of faith *have power to place* us where we can receive a sense of the presence of God" (63).

Christian practices are a means of grace, and they are not, as Serene
Jones so effectively communicates, duties we undertake to win approval
from God.[57] Rather, again according to Dykstra, "They are *patterns of communal action that create openings in our lives* where the grace, mercy, and presence of God may be made known to us. They are *places* where the power of
God is experienced. In the end, *these are not ultimately our practices but forms of
participation in the practice of God*."[58] Christian practices embody convictions; they are intentional activities that are imbued with understanding.
Participation in the practices "shapes people in certain ways, developing
in them certain habits, virtues and capacities of mind and spirit."[59] Christian practices are a means by which the Holy Spirit transforms and shapes
people. Like strong theories of conversion, it is encountering the ever-
active God in the midst of the practices of the Christian faith that takes
what is there and turns it toward Christ.

The practices of the Christian faith have a **witnessing** aspect. They
not only witness to our beliefs or "imply certain beliefs about ourselves,
our neighbors and God." Christian practices are the means by which the
life and witness of the community are incarnated in the world. I hesitate to
consider the practices, as articulated by the Valparaiso conversation,
missional, as I will explain later, because the practices conversation is yet
to give adequate attention to the gospel, church, and culture triad; explore
multicultural perspectives; or embrace and build upon the idea that God
is, by nature, a missionary God. This is, of course, a contribution that this
book hopes to make.

Positively, however, since Christian practices are not about therapeutic, moralistic, privatistic, and inward-looking spirituality, practices, according to this discussion, both anchor a way of life for individuals and
communities and spill over into a wounded world. In the words of Bass
and Dykstra, "Practices are filled with meaning, and the meaning goes far
beyond our own spiritual life to touch all the suffering of humanity.
Taking part in Christian practices can cultivate qualities we did not have
before and open our eyes and hearts to the activity of God's Spirit in the
wider world. This may satisfy some of the yearning with which we began,

---

57. Serene Jones, "Graced Practices: Excellence and Freedom in the Christian Life," in
Practicing Theology.

58. Dykstra, *Growing in the Life*, 66, emphasis mine.

59. Bass and Dykstra, "Christian Practices," 254.

but it also introduces yearning of a deeper sort — a yearning for divine justice and peace for all."[60]

While it is clear that there is a witnessing aspect to Christian practices, witness is not clearly defined in the Valparaiso literature. However, witness seems to be related to becoming responsive to the work and movement of God's reconciling love. As the literature suggests, all practices are communal and intentional responses to "God's active presence for the life of the world."[61] Woven together, Christian practices "bear witness to God's forgiving, re-creating activity for the world."[62] If the church is missionary by her very nature, and if the practices constitute the church's way of life, in what ways is the purpose of the church evident in the practices of the faith as articulated in the Valparaiso conversation? This is an underdeveloped theme in the discussion, and one the missional theologian deems vitally important.

Christian Practices Come to Focus in Worship

Paradigmatic for Christian practices is worship; or, as many involved in the practices discussion would agree, "all the practices of daily life come to a focus in worship."[63] As Craig Dykstra has made clear, there is really only one practice, and that is the practice of worship. Worship is the practice of the entire Christian life, and to practice Christian faith is to practice a way of life that is a life of worship — a life of thanksgiving and praise to God. However, since a whole way of life is too difficult to talk about, it is helpful to break it down into the contingent practices that together weave a way of life. Worship, or life in dependence and reliance upon the God of life, is the whole of which all these particular practices are a part.[64]

While the practices addressed in *Practicing Our Faith* may be found to some degree in the life of any congregation, the authors believe that it is in the shared gestures, words, and images of the worship service, in their liturgical expression, that these Christian practices are gathered to address every aspect of the human condition.[65] Christian worship, especially the

---

60. Dorothy C. Bass, *Practicing Our Faith*, 200-201.
61. Dorothy C. Bass, *Practicing Our Faith*, 5.
62. L. Gregory Jones, "Forgiveness," in *Practicing Our Faith*, 140.
63. Bass and Dykstra, "Christian Practices," 254.
64. Bass, Dykstra, and Wuthnow, "Practicing Christian Faith."
65. Honoring the body, hospitality, household economics, saying yes and saying no,

liturgy, "distills the Christian meaning of the practices and holds them up for the whole community to see."[66] In this liturgical expression, the many practices are related to one another by the coherence that arises from the Trinitarian God who is worshiped.

In his early engagement with Christian practices, Dykstra offered worship as the first practice.[67] Presenting a broad understanding of worship, not confined to its liturgical expression, Dykstra promoted worship as the paradigmatic, central, governing, and animating practice of the Christian life. Worship, in this broad sense, is the point of everything the Christian does. Worship is all the practices *in nuce*. In this sense, worship is "an overarching master practice rather than one practice among many."[68] In the same way, argues Tom Long, "Christian worship is the master practice from which and toward which all flow and come into focus." Drawing on Geoffrey Wainwright, Long continues, "Worship is the point of concentration in which the whole of the Christian life comes into ritual focus."[69] According to the *Practicing Our Faith* discussion, every practice is embedded to some degree in the act of liturgical Christian worship.

In this discussion, however, the service of worship, baptism, and the Lord's Supper are not considered practices per se partly because they are not large-scale communal ways of being in the world that address a specific human condition. Liturgical worship addresses all of them. These sacraments are "more normative and more encompassing than any given practice can be."[70] They are "liturgical summation[s] of all the Christian practices," or practices in "crystalline form" that "ritually [sketch] the contours of a whole new life."[71]

---

keeping Sabbath, testimony, discernment, shaping communities, forgiveness, healing, dying well, and singing our lives.

66. Dorothy C. Bass, *Practicing Our Faith*, 9.

67. Presbyterian Church (U.S.A.), Theology and Worship Ministry Unit, and Presbyterian Church (U.S.A.), General Assembly, *Growing in the Life of Christian Faith: Commended to the Church for Information and Study* (Louisville: Theology and Worship Ministry Unit, Presbyterian Church [U.S.A.], 1989), 27.

68. Dorothy C. Bass, "What Is a Christian Practice?"

69. Bass, Dykstra, and Wuthnow, "Practicing Christian Faith."

70. Dorothy C. Bass, "What Is a Christian Practice?"

71. Dykstra and Bass, "A Theological Understanding," 30-31.

*Serene Jones's "Graced Practices" as an Example of the Possibilities and
Limitations of the Practices Discussion, So Far*

Serene Jones's "Graced Practices: Excellence and Freedom in the Christian
Life" provides an excellent example of the possibilities of the Valparaiso
Project's approach to Christian practices and embodies some of the limitations and underdeveloped aspects of the discussion. Positively, Jones's
unique contribution to the discussion is that she offers a glimpse into the
discernment process of a Millennial Committee in one particular congregation and demonstrates how that process draws into consideration many
of the other practices considered in *Practicing Our Faith*. She offers insight-
ful commentary on how doctrines and practices relate to one another.
Moreover, Jones draws upon her own Reformed tradition's exploration of
the work of God's grace in justification and sanctification to offer the paradigm of "adorned in freedom" as a basic posture that Christians should
take toward the practices that are constitutive of their congregational life.
Jones is addressing the question, "How are we saved by grace and what
does this say about the shape of our daily patterns of living, our collective
and individual practices?"[72]

Her approach highlights all the aforementioned aspects of Christian
practices. Historically, her practices have been preserved, practiced, and
passed on within the Reformed tradition. Calvin serves as her interlocutor. The self-understanding of her own United Church of Christ congregation has been significantly shaped in doctrine and practice by this tradition, since the practices that she engages in all emanate from the narrative
core of the Reformed faith. These practices carry within them a history
that has been inherited and is being shaped by one congregation to fit
present circumstances for the sake of the future. The practice of discernment that Jones describes is one that "the people of faith have followed for
centuries."[73]

This practice of discernment, and the related practices, are social in
nature. As Jones makes clear, the practice of discernment is not novel or
unique to her congregation. The process of listening and envisioning is a
community exercise that has been passed down through generations of
believers and addresses patterns of corporate action. While intending to

---

72. Jones, "Graced Practices," 57.
73. Jones, "Graced Practices," 53.

demonstrate how a specific constellation of practices can be understood through the lenses of sanctification and justification, her congregation's plan to develop a women's spirituality group was also an example of how these practices engage and include a whole community. The practices of Sabbath keeping, honoring the body, hospitality, and discernment imagined by the Millennial Committee involve child care, an intentional space, a structure and shape. Furthermore, the process of discernment is undertaken with one hand on the Scriptures and the other on Christian texts and the insights of contemporary theologians.[74]

There is a universal aspect to the practices that Jones discusses. The practices mentioned address overwork, "oppressive dynamics that accompany being women in today's world," the need to feel welcomed and cared for, and the need for support and guidance in negotiating the complexities of life. While finding unique expression in her own community, Jones presents universal concerns that are the interest of specific Christian practices.

At the same time, while addressing universal concerns, the practices that Jones and company consider are intimately local. They are the practices of a small congregation in downtown New Haven, Connecticut, in a "poor but thriving inner-city environment."[75] This congregation is a "Word-centered, confessional community"[76] that is embarking on specific projects in a particular way. A distinctive contribution to an overall understanding of Christian practices emerges from this setting. From the standpoint of sanctifying grace, Christian practices "are the things that Christians do as their lives are conformed to patterns of living that embody God's will, patterns embedded in the Law and manifest in the life of Christ, patterns of holiness — *sanctus*."[77] From this perspective, practices are called to be excellent. On the other hand, from the standpoint of justifying grace, Christian practices have "relativized soteriological significance."[78] That is to say, while the practices of the church deal with the forming and shaping work of grace in the lives of believers, practices themselves do not offer salvation and should not be considered normative in any one particular expression. Therefore, practices are afforded a cer-

74. Jones, "Graced Practices," 54.
75. Jones, "Graced Practices," 51.
76. Jones, "Graced Practices," 56.
77. Jones, "Graced Practices," 60.
78. Jones, "Graced Practices," 65.

tain creative and responsive freedom that issues from a joyful response to God's grace and can be evaluated for effectiveness in terms of their witnessing function.

Jones states very clearly, along the lines of Dykstra, that the practices have a certain epistemological or conversional aspect to them. Building on her argument that doctrines are as much "dramatic scripts" and "imaginative landscapes" as they are propositional statements of belief, Jones explains that "practices are not just things we do in light of doctrines; practices are what we become as we are set in motion in the space of doctrine."[79] There is an interplay between beliefs and practices, an epistemological and conversional movement, such that beliefs are determinate of practices and practices are determinate of beliefs. On the one hand, it can be argued that it is what one intends, what one believes, that makes a practice Christian. On the other hand, the practices will inform how one understands and imagines doctrines, often in ways that are "unconscious" or "nonconscious" and not necessarily apparent to the practitioner.[80]

Finally, one can discern in Jones's essay that the practices of the church have a witnessing aspect in that they witness to God's grace at work in the world. At least some of the practices force the church to live eccentrically, but all practices are "enactments of our freedom"[81] that are "performed as witness."[82] Practices are free to do this because they are unencumbered by soteriological weight, that is, they do not contribute to our justification and therefore can be evaluated for "practical effectiveness and contextual appropriateness" as they "witness to the world of God's grace."[83] The potential here for a missional theologically conceived notion of Christian practices is great; however, Jones, in the brevity of her essay, is only able to link the witnessing aspect of practices to the dynamic relationship between the doctrines of sanctification and justification and leaves the missional theological significance of practices underdeveloped.

Jones does well to look at the practices through the lenses of her own Reformed tradition, and with the aid of Calvin, offers some penetrating insights into how justification and sanctification are interrelated as well as

79. Jones, "Graced Practices," 75.
80. Jones, "Graced Practices," 75-77.
81. Jones, "Graced Practices," 73.
82. Jones, "Graced Practices," 67.
83. Jones, "Graced Practices," 67.

how their significance for Christian practices may be considered in terms of excellence and freedom. The problem, from the standpoint of missional theology, is that Calvin debated Cardinal Sadoleto in a "Christian world."[84] The Christendom paradigm was operative when Calvin worked out his doctrine. He was challenging the idea that people are saved by participating in an unerring church's faith and worship and that the process of justification must include good works. His culture was Christian, and citizenship in society meant membership in the church — the question was whether that church would be Catholic or Protestant. Theology written in response to such a context provides little guidance to a people trying to think in terms of their missional vocation. Calvin responded faithfully in his context, but could never have anticipated or addressed ours.

David Bosch offers insight into Calvin's cultural setting. Bosch notes that reforming the church was the consuming, primary goal of Reformation Protestants. Besides, external persecution and internal strife left little energy for organization for mission. Furthermore, while Catholics had extended colonial empires and were consistently encountering the unevangelized, Protestants remained largely landlocked and without contact with non-Christians. Finally, having abandoned monasticism, Protestants had jettisoned an important missionary organ.[85]

As I have already noted, there is, positively, the connection of the practices to the ongoing redemptive work of God in the world, but little is said about the nature of the community that is gathered, built up, and sent to participate in that work. What Dykstra will call "contemporary developments in Reformed theology,"[86] the work of those I have termed the progenitors of missional theology, is never considered by the greater Valparaiso conversation. The hub of worship, around which the practices cohere, is a worship that is lacking an ecclesiology that is clear about the nature of the church.

The weakness of the *Practicing Our Faith* conversation, and why it is incomplete in the eyes of the missional theologian, is that it fails to take ac-

84. John C. Olin, ed., *A Reformation Debate: John Calvin and Jacopo Sadoleto* (Grand Rapids: Baker, 1976).

85. David Jacobus Bosch, *Transforming Mission: Paradigm Shifts in Theology of Mission*, American Society of Missiology Series, no. 16 (Maryknoll, N.Y.: Orbis, 1991), 245.

86. Presbyterian Church (U.S.A.), Theology and Worship Ministry Unit, and Presbyterian Church (U.S.A.), General Assembly, *Growing in the Life*, 26.

count of the nature and purpose of the church; the interaction between gospel, church, and culture represented by Hunsberger's triad; and the multicultural perspective. Just as Jones, perhaps due to the brevity of her essay and perhaps due to its structure and use of Calvin as interlocutor, fails to lift out how justification and sanctification express themselves through calling, that is, vocation, the Valparaiso conversation fails to adequately consider vocation. Karl Barth's theological project is particularly helpful in this regard because the doctrines of justification, sanctification, and vocation together constitute his doctrine of reconciliation. In Barth's opinion, vocation is what keeps the theological doctrines of justification and sanctification from being malnourished and allows us to avoid the trap of focusing on the benefits of salvation to the neglect of witness or mission. Until vocation is considered, the doctrines of justification and sanctification run the risk of focusing inwardly on the benefits of grace to the individual and the community of faith or contribute to the tendency to separate worship from mission.

If, as Jones says, "the doctrines of justification and sanctification gave us a distinctive orientation toward all our practices," then how might that orientation toward the practices be altered if the doctrine of calling or vocation were added as an essential element of the doctrine of reconciliation, or as Jones puts it, grace at work? In other words, if sanctification calls for excellence in practices and justification calls forth freedom, what does vocation call for? How would the perspective of the missional church change the inner meaning or dynamic of the practices? How would it change how the practices are understood to function in the congregation? What practices would the missional theologian add to the list offered in *Practicing Our Faith?*

The question is, if the thesis of the missional church were accepted, what would that missional understanding bring out of this conversation that is mutually enriching? While Dykstra is certainly a partner in the framing of the Valparaiso conversation about Christian practices, there remains in Dykstra's works an untapped resource for moving the practices discussion into an important conversation with missional theology about the nature of the church and the implications of that reality for Christian practices.

CHAPTER FOUR

Craig Dykstra's Conception
of Christian Practices

Having introduced the *Practicing Our Faith* discussion of Christian practices in the previous chapter, having uncovered its foundational assumptions and exposited its definition of Christian practices, I will now narrow my attention to Craig Dykstra's theology and appropriation of Christian practices. The purpose of this chapter is to suggest how some of his works and ideas, some that have proven fundamental to the practices discussion and some that have not received adequate expression in the *Practicing Our Faith* conversation so far, may provide a framework for initiating a dialogue about missional Christian practices. I am not suggesting that Dykstra's conception of practices will provide the foundation for a missional understanding of practices. I am claiming that Dykstra is open to a missional reading of his work and is willing to engage in such a conversation about how missional church theology and the contemporary Christian practices discussions relate and what they reveal about one another.

It is my contention that by attending to the practices discussion, and particularly Craig Dykstra's conception of Christian practices, missional theology will be able to draw new fuel for a timely conversation about the nature of the church's witness, its congregational discipleship, and its theological education.

Dykstra and Christian Practices

Craig Dykstra is centrally important to the Valparaiso Project/*Practicing Our Faith* discussion about Christian practices on at least two levels. First, Dykstra lent his support to the project as the vice president and then senior vice president of religion for the Lilly Endowment. In this role he allocated the financial resources necessary for enduring, focused study on the topic. Second, and equally significant, Dykstra invested his rich background as a practical theologian in the discussion. As the Thomas W. Synnott Professor of Christian Education at Princeton Theological Seminary, Dykstra had developed seminars in practical theology that challenged the direction of the discipline and entered him into the contest between those who promulgated the clerical paradigm, an approach to practical theology in which all attention is given to the practices of the clergy, and those who, like himself, insisted that theological education was for the benefit of the practice of the ordinary Christian. Dykstra has continued to pursue intellectually his thoughts on practical theology and Christian education through the projects funded by Lilly. In particular, Dykstra's body of work is important to this book because it opens the practices discussion to a missional perspective that is latent in his work and especially in some of his early writings.

After overviewing Dykstra's contributions to the practices discussion, this chapter will draw out his ecclesiology and demonstrate how it is grounded in his reception and application of Edward Farley's notion of *ecclesia* and in the ecclesial reflections of some of the incipient missional theologians. Finally, I will suggest how Dykstra and the *Practicing Our Faith* discussion could join with missional theologians to refine an important conversation about missionally informed Christian practices.

How did Dykstra's theology of practices develop? On the one hand, Dykstra's whole approach to the practices discussion could be distilled into the simplicity of the early church document the *Didache:* "There are two ways, one of life and one of death; and between the two ways there is a great difference."[1] He simply believes that there is available, in the practices of the Christian tradition, the wisdom, guidance, and power to live the way of life that is pleasing and faithful to God. In his own writings,

---

1. Cyril C. Richardson, ed., *Early Christian Fathers*, Library of Christian Classics, vol. 1 (New York: Touchstone, 1996), 171.

Dykstra has made the notion of practices central to his reflection on the discipleship and theological education of the church.

On the other hand, Dykstra's approach to the practices is as complex as his conversation partners. His notion of Christian practices was shaped by his reflection on Christian ethics and the important work of his dissertation regarding the moral life of the church, specifically his attempt to find an alternative to Lawrence Kohlberg's juridical ethics as a basis for understanding Christian moral formation. It was refined through his interaction with James Fowler and their contestation over the very definition of faith and the question of which approach to faith development is adequate. It was articulated in his work with the Presbyterian church when he continued his practical engagement with faith development and tied it most intentionally to a theology of Christian practices. It was nuanced over the course of a professorship during which he took seriously the call of Farley to challenge the so-called clerical paradigm and to consider how the community of faith gives a particular emphasis to Christian practices as related to the *ecclesia*. It was given structure through his discovery and engagement of MacIntyre's *After Virtue*. MacIntyre helped him to articulate his oft-quoted philosophy of practice in "Reconceiving Practice." Finally, the Valparaiso conversation and its associated conferences provided the context for important exchanges about the nature of practices and built upon the foundation that he and Dorothy Bass had laid.

Michael Warren, in his introductory words to a chapter cowritten by Dykstra and Bass on Christian practices entitled "Christian Practices and Congregational Education in the Faith," correctly recognizes "the seeds of Dykstra's ideas on practice" in his *Vision and Character*.[2] Dykstra's dissertation, later revised and published as *Vision and Character: A Christian Educator's Alternative to Kohlberg*, represented his promotion of visional ethics as an alternative to juridical ethics as a foundation for moral education in the church. His important question is: If we are training for Christian morality, then how might the resources of the Christian faith and the Christian community of faith be brought to bear on our approach to morality?[3] After critiquing Kohlberg's somewhat mechanical and abstract developmental

2. Dorothy C. Bass and Craig R. Dykstra, "Christian Practices and Congregational Education in Faith," in *Changing Churches: The Local Church and the Structures of Change*, ed. Michael Warren (Portland, Oreg.: Pastoral Press, 2000), 247.

3. Craig R. Dykstra, *Vision and Character: A Christian Educator's Alternative to Kohlberg* (New York: Paulist, 1981), 3.

theory of morality, Dykstra argues that our moral decisions and choices are grounded in the "quality of our perception" or our vision of the world.[4] He challenges Kohlberg's unexamined commitment to the modern scientific worldview and offers instead a vision of the world that accepts revelation, mystery, and a kind of knowledge that is a gift to be witnessed to rather than wrenched from our circumstances. Dykstra challenges the privileged position that Kohlberg's worldview affords to notions like empirical facts, the universal viewpoint, the autonomous individual, the idea that people are clusters of unrelated faculties, the tendency of the modern worldview to separate facts from values, and the centrality and supremacy of human reason. Instead, Dykstra posits a vision of reality that makes room for the transcendent, recognizes that people are unitary beings, and accepts that all knowledge involves faith commitments of some sort.

The development of such a worldview or vision, explains Dykstra, necessitates a community that is shaped by the formative disciplines of repentance, prayer, and service. As Dykstra unfolds it, "These three are the fundamental disciplines by which the moral lives of Christians grow. They are the disciplines of discipleship, and through them we move more and more into a position where the mysteries of reality can be revealed to us . . . we put ourselves out of the way so God can do God's work in us."[5] The language and the rituals of the community both reflect and shape their vision. Though situated in a discussion about Christian formation, this vision of discipleship could be easily related to mission, broadly conceived, or ministry in the world, because Dykstra describes discipleship in terms of "active engagement in the world as persons formed by Christian faith."[6] Within this community, the disciplines provide a means through which people can put themselves in the position where God changes them. Drawing on Diogenes Allen, Dykstra argues that the disciplines help us to "get into the condition which allows us to perceive mysteries."[7] Eventually the language of "disciplines" will give way to the discussion of "practices," but it is important to note that Dykstra, whether he is addressing disciplines or practices, is always addressing Christian discipleship.[8]

---

4. Dykstra, *Vision and Character*, 23.

5. Dykstra, *Vision and Character*, 105.

6. Dykstra, *Vision and Character*, 90.

7. Diogenes Allen, *Between Two Worlds: A Guide for Those Who Are Beginning to Be Religious* (Atlanta: John Knox, 1977), 14-15.

8. "But Christians have historically understood the formation of the moral life as for-

Dykstra's own understanding of practices, in the next phase of his academic development, continued to develop from an apologetic for a few rather churchly disciplines to a more refined notion of practices. Dykstra first encountered *After Virtue* six months after *Vision and Character* was published. He found it helpful for framing what he was attempting to communicate in talking about disciplines. Having previously defined disciplines as those ordered activities that put us in a position where we can perceive mystery, Dykstra continued to develop the concept while offering his first use of the term "practices" in his contribution to *Faith Development and Fowler* (1986). After defining faith as a participatory response, namely, "Faith is appropriate and intentional participation in the redemptive activity of God,"[9] he adds that knowing how to respond in faith requires "learning the skills and habits and ways of thinking and behaving and feeling that are involved in a way of living that is an appropriate response."[10] While disputing Fowler's claim that growth in faith may somehow be determined by discrete, incrementally advancing stages of human development, Dykstra offers an alternative. Growth in faith will not necessarily be by means of progressive development with irreversible stages. Instead, "particular kinds of practices will be necessary in order to grow in faith."[11] He lists some of the practices (worship, study of sacred texts, the engagement of certain disciplines [meditation or fasting], fellowship, and activities of service to the world). Then he continues, "Though these practices are in part expressions of the faith that is growing, they are not just that. They are also experiences through which growth in faith takes place; and they are necessary ones for that growth. Through such practices, people's knowledge of, capacity for, and patterns of response to God are being formed."[12]

His work on the Council on Theology and Culture and on the study

---

mation in discipleship. To be a disciple is to be an adherent of the way of Christ. It is to be a follower of his, and to have one's life formed through the strenuous discipline of going where he went, looking at things the way he did, trusting as he trusted, making ourselves vulnerable as he was vulnerable . . . the way to grow morally is to undertake the discipline of becoming disciples." Dykstra, *Vision and Character*, 90.

9. Craig R. Dykstra, "What Is Faith? An Experiment in the Hypothetical Mode," in *Faith Development and Fowler*, ed. Craig R. Dykstra, Sharon Parks, and James W. Fowler (Birmingham, Ala.: Religious Education Press, 1986), 55.

10. Dykstra, "What Is Faith?" 56.

11. Dykstra, "What Is Faith?" 60.

12. Dykstra, "What Is Faith?" 60.

commissioned by the Advisory Council on Discipleship and Worship of the Presbyterian Church (U.S.A.) on "faith development and the Reformed tradition" from 1985 to 1989 reflects another stage in Dykstra's contribution to the contemporary practices discussion.[13] The fruit of that study, *Growing in the Life of Christian Faith,* carries in embryonic and recognizable form the current practices discussion. Two important premises of the study are that the Christian faith begins with God's active presence with and for the world and that there are available in the fundamental practices of the Reformed tradition what we need to live the life of faith. Building upon this foundation, Dykstra suggests that over the course of history the church has come to rely upon certain central disciplines or practices of the faith that aid in nurturing the faith of the church. The shift from "disciplines" language to "practices" language occurs with the aid of MacIntyre's definition of practices from *After Virtue.* While he does not offer any sustained reflection on MacIntyre's concept in *Growing in the Life of Christian Faith,* Dykstra does mention MacIntyre in a footnote when clarifying the newly introduced concept of "practice":

> A "practice" is an ongoing shared activity of a community of people that partly defines and partly makes them who they are. A more complex and precise definition is provided and discussed by Alasdair MacIntyre in *After Virtue.* . . . The term "discipline" is virtually synonymous with practice, but we use both because several connotations of discipline are helpful in our context, particularly as we think of "spiritual disciplines" and "church discipline." Disciplines are practices and all practices are disciplined.[14]

Most importantly for connecting the practices discussion to the nature and purpose of the church and missional theology, Dykstra calls

13. The report of the task force, of which Dykstra was the writer, can be found in Presbyterian Church (U.S.A.), Theology and Worship Ministry Unit, and Presbyterian Church (U.S.A.), General Assembly, *Growing in the Life of Christian Faith: Commended to the Church for Information and Study* (Louisville: Theology and Worship Ministry Unit, Presbyterian Church [U.S.A.], 1989). Portions of the report were published ten years later under his own name as representative of his understanding of Christian practices and his contribution to the practices discussion. See Craig R. Dykstra, *Growing in the Life of Faith: Education and Christian Practices,* 1st ed. (Louisville: Geneva Press, 1999).

14. Presbyterian Church (U.S.A.), Theology and Worship Ministry Unit, and Presbyterian Church (U.S.A.), General Assembly, *Growing in the Life of Christian Faith,* 40-41 n. 40.

upon what he terms "contemporary developments in Reformed theology" that help his reader to understand "the place of the church and its practices in the economy of God's grace."[15] These "contemporary developments" are associated with Jürgen Moltmann's insight about the church's participation in the history of God's dealings with the world,[16] with Barth's notion that the Christian life is "existence in the execution of this [commission],"[17] and with the Confession of 1967 (C67) and the commentary on C67 offered by Edward Dowey Jr. Dowey suggests that Israel's holiness is inextricably related to her being chosen for a purpose. The Israelites were not holy because of their moral condition, but instead because "they were chosen for a special mission in the world. The same is true of the church and each of its members."[18]

While at Princeton Dykstra developed seminars in practical theology and disputed the direction of the discipline. Dykstra insisted that theological education is for the benefit of the practice of the ordinary Christian, and he challenged those who felt that theological education should submit to a "clerical paradigm" — again, an approach to preparing theological students for the ministry in which all attention is given to the practices of the clergy. The relationship of pastor to congregant is not an expert/client relationship. Thus a strong theology of the laity is essential to the theology of practices as conceived by Dykstra, as it is also to the missional church conversation. Fundamentally, argues Dykstra, we are all participants in the *ecclesia* — a word that, drawing on Farley's writings, has more to do with a community's participation in the continuing reconciling work of God than with one's membership in an institution. The pastors or

15. Presbyterian Church (U.S.A.), Theology and Worship Ministry Unit, and Presbyterian Church (U.S.A.), General Assembly, *Growing in the Life of Christian Faith*, 26.

16. Jürgen Moltmann, *The Church in the Power of the Spirit: A Contribution to Messianic Ecclesiology* (Minneapolis: Fortress, 1993), 64-65.

17. Karl Barth, *The Doctrine of Reconciliation*, vol. IV/3.2 of *Church Dogmatics*, ed. G. W. Bromiley and T. F. Torrance (Edinburgh: T. & T. Clark, 1962), 573-74. Note that I earlier suggested that the term "commission" is a more accurate term than "task" for relating Barth's understanding of calling in his doctrine of vocation. This section on the vocation of the individual is expanded on pages 795-830 to include and explain the "[Commission] of the Community."

18. Edward A. Dowey and United Presbyterian Church in the U.S.A., *A Commentary on the Confession of 1967 and an Introduction to the Book of Confessions* (Philadelphia: Westminster, 1968), 90. Quoted in Presbyterian Church (U.S.A.), Theology and Worship Ministry Unit, and Presbyterian Church (U.S.A.), General Assembly, *Growing in the Life of Christian Faith*, 16.

clergy must organize the political ordering of the community in such a way as to foster the life and faith of the ordinary Christian and to increase the congregants' own agency through the practices of the faith "that constitute being the church."[19] The life of the community, then, is marked by certain practices, and these practices are understood in a particular way that challenges what Dykstra understood to be the prevailing notion of practices.

Dykstra later fills out the list of disciplines or practices that had appeared in *Vision and Character* and was expanded in *Growing in the Life of Christian Faith* by the use of MacIntyre's notion of practices in "Reconceiving Practice."

A close reading of "Reconceiving Practice" uncovers the impact of Farley and MacIntyre on Dykstra's thought about Christian practice. Dykstra argues that theological education is hampered by an understanding of practice borrowed from a broader cultural and socially prevalent understanding of practice in which a practice is "individualistic, technological, ahistorical and abstract."[20] In this case a practice is a strategic and patterned action, carried out by professionals to effect change in other persons by using social scientific theories and outside of larger moral considerations. "Practice" in theological education, Dykstra argued, followed this same pattern and was largely understood to be focused on the actions of clergy along the lines of the "clerical paradigm" that Farley described. Practical theology, which was concerned with the practice of congregations, became centered on preparing professionals for carrying out the duties of church life. Practice cannot mean the technical application of a theory or a procedure to a duty outside of a wider theological framework or *habitus*,[21] argues Dykstra, because then all the various academic disciplines become "distorted, fragmented, and overly dependent upon and

19. Presbyterian Church (U.S.A.), Theology and Worship Ministry Unit, and Presbyterian Church (U.S.A.), General Assembly, *Growing in the Life of Christian Faith*, 28. By the phrase "constitute being the church," Dykstra means something like embody, instantiate, or make visible the church, and not to formally establish and call into being the church. He understands, as a faithful Reformed theologian, that the church is constituted by the action of God and not by human initiative.

20. Craig R. Dykstra, "Reconceiving Practice," in *Shifting Boundaries: Contextual Approaches to the Structure of Theological Education*, ed. Barbara G. Wheeler and Edward Farley (Louisville: Westminster John Knox, 1991), 35.

21. The wisdom appropriate to the life of a believer.

conformed to university disciplines and their secular, Enlightenment assumptions; and their own point, or *telos*, as a dimension of theological study is obscured."[22] A particular view of the world is implicated in the practice.

In contradistinction to the prevailing, utilitarian notion of practice, Dykstra builds upon MacIntyre's well-known definition of social practices to offer an alternate understanding of practice that is communal and cooperative — an understanding of practices that considers the "goods inherent" to a practice or the "internal goods" of a practice. An understanding of practice that bears within it fundamentally individualistic, technological, and ahistorical assumptions cannot provide adequate direction for a way of life — at least not a way of life consistent with Christian understandings of what it means to live in response to God's promise and call.[23] Dykstra embraced MacIntyre because MacIntyre's approach to practices helped him to frame a challenge to the prevailing utilitarian and technical rationale for practice, take seriously the issue of the formative community, and build constructively on an approach that could be more consistent with his vision of practical theology and theological education.

Dykstra's next move, therefore, was to build upon MacIntyre's understanding of social practice to make it more suitable for Christian practice. "In order to discern the significance of practice for Christian life," explains Dykstra, "we have needed to move beyond MacIntyre's historical-moral claim to make epistemological-theological suggestions."[24] In other words, Dykstra, extending MacIntyre through Farley, is suggesting that beyond certain "goods" that are only accessible to people when they engage in a practice, there are, furthermore, certain realities related to a palpable reality, a knowledge of God, that becomes known only in the context of certain practices. This knowledge is the encounter with a reality that is otherwise beyond our ken. The practices themselves offer us a place of encounter or "the conditions under which" this new knowledge arises.[25] Dykstra, an astute Reformed theologian, is careful to add that practices do not allow us to manipulate revelation. Revelation, knowledge of God, and

---

22. Dykstra, "Reconceiving Practice," 59 n. 1.

23. Dorothy Bass explains in her preface to *Growing in the Life of Faith* that Dykstra appropriated MacIntyre's concept of practices yet nuanced it with theological themes from the Reformed tradition. Dykstra, *Growing in the Life of Faith*, xiii.

24. Dykstra, "Reconceiving Practice," 47.

25. Dykstra, "Reconceiving Practice," 46 and 49.

the things of God are always a gift. Nonetheless, certain practices have proven "efficacious" in the long history of the church.

In Farley's terms, Dykstra is arguing that "social relationships mediate realities [through] their capacity to effect new powers of perceptiveness."[26] Dykstra is suggesting that Farley is correct when he argues that pre-conscious apprehensions attend "participation in ecclesia's intersubjectivity."[27] Most significantly, Dykstra is echoing Farley's conclusion that *ecclesia*'s intersubjectivity is related to a redemptive modification of human existence and makes us cognizant of our responsibility as Christians in the world. Dykstra posits the following question: "Suppose that through participation in practices of Christian life, the community of faith comes continually to awareness of and participation in the creative and redemptive activity of God in the world."[28] The practices of the Christian life awaken our commitment to the redemptive work of God beyond the intramural concerns of the church. It follows that, since Dykstra's understanding of practices is dependent upon a community defined by its participation in the ongoing redemptive work of God in the world, his conception of practices necessitates a rethinking of his inherited Reformed ecclesiology. As Albert Winn suggests, "The time-honored *notae ecclesiae*, the marks of the church, are the preaching of the word and the administration of the sacraments. . . . But if we are on the right track in these studies, then surely the preeminent mark of the church is engagement in mission to the world."[29]

---

26. Dykstra, "Reconceiving Practice," 46.

27. Edward Farley, *Ecclesial Man: A Social Phenomenology of Faith and Reality* (Philadelphia: Fortress, 1975), 213. For Farley, *ecclesia* is the determinate social world of Christian faith — it involves *intersubjectivity* or the "interpersonal structure which exists pre-consciously and which is already prior to any actual relationship or dialogue as their condition" (94). This intersubjectivity is determinate (it provides what Berger terms a plausibility structure or a worldview) and has a preconscious mediatory function. What is seen and how it is seen are impacted by this determinate intersubjectivity. In *ecclesia* this determinate intersubjectivity is marked by a redemptive modification of existence. Faith requires a language of its own, a community, and the *ecclesia*, which includes the determinate intersubjectivity (universal) and an ever-changing institutionalization (local). Farley suggests that for primitive Christianity, "to 'believe in Jesus Christ' meant to enter into a new form of corporate existence, and with that entrance began participation in its co-intentionalities which are directed beyond itself to the stranger" (172).

28. Dykstra, "Reconceiving Practice," 49-50.

29. Albert Curry Winn, *A Sense of Mission: Guidance from the Gospel of John* (Philadelphia: Westminster, 1981), 52-53.

Dykstra's Ecclesiology and the Practices

Dykstra's ecclesiology is particularly important for connecting his discussion of practices with the missional theology conversation. The point about ecclesiology made above is not simply that the disciplines or practices must be connected to some sort of transformative community that both reflects and shapes a new vision of reality. The point is that this community, as the Christian community, has certain characteristics that mark it as the body of Christ, as the ministry of the Holy Spirit, as the work of the Trinity. This church is not defined along the lines of the Reformed attributes of pure preaching, right administration of the sacraments, and the exercise of church discipline. Nor is it defined in terms of traditional understandings of the classic *notae* of oneness, holiness, catholicity, and apostolicity. The church is defined by its service to the ongoing work of God in the world. This *ad extra* orientation is, for Dykstra, "the very dynamics of what it means to be the church" to such a degree that the church that does not attempt to incorporate into its fellowship the enemies and strangers of life is not the church.[30] These are vitally important insights to the missional theologian. Unfortunately, it is difficult to discern how this missional orientation functions very strongly in Dykstra's main body of work or in the *Practicing Our Faith* conversation. I will take up this issue in the subsequent chapter.

The most concise statement of Dykstra's ecclesiology can be found in his inaugural lecture at Princeton Theological Seminary in which he offered some reflections on how his work on Christian formation is related to his understanding of ecclesiology. "My own work is taking a turn toward more explicit and systematic attention to the church," he reflects, "wondering what we really mean when we use that word and what the actual reality of it suggests for the church's education ministry."[31]

---

30. Dykstra, *Vision and Character*, 114-15. In full, with italics added for emphasis — "As we follow him, we see that we cannot be the church and remain a closed system of intimate and exclusive social relationships through which we are protected from the world. To the extent that we actually are being transformed in repentance, prayer, and service, we find that we must continually strive to rupture our own boundaries. *The church is just not the church* except as it seeks to incorporate within its mutuality enemies and strangers. *Its repentance, prayer, and service is for all people, for the world as such, and not just for other Christians.* In the church *we are impelled by the very dynamics of what it means to be the church* to meet enemies and strangers of our lives."

31. Craig R. Dykstra, "No Longer Strangers: The Church and Its Educational Ministry,"

Working exegetically with Ephesians 2:19-20 and drawing on the insights from the seminal missional theologians Barth and Moltmann, Dykstra makes a case that rather than being focused inward, the church is gathered together and formed in response to the prior redemptive action of God in such a way that we are no longer strangers to God's redemptive presence in the world. To believe in the church, as the Apostles' Creed affirms, is to believe that in the mundane assembly of believers the continuing work of Christ through the Holy Spirit takes place. It is this participation in the ongoing redemptive activity of God that defines the church for Dykstra. In fact, both faith and mission (that which is often wrongly divided into the internal and external life of the church) are similarly defined for Dykstra as participation in the redemptive activity of God.[32]

The church as the dwelling place of God in the Spirit should not be conceived in spatial, institutional, or socio-structural terms. The church as the dwelling place of God is a dynamic, active, and historical reality; "a work, an activity."[33] It is where God is active; it is wherever God is carrying out God's work of redemption in the world for the sake of the world. And, in the tradition of Barth, the world is defined for Dykstra as not merely the world, but as the world that God is for. Succinctly, and in his own words, "in Christ by the Spirit in the church, we are being called into, led into, built into participation in the ongoing redemptive activity of God in the world."[34]

With respect to the practices, Dykstra argues that growth in the

---

in *Theological Perspectives on Christian Formation: A Reader on Theology and Christian Education*, ed. Jeff Astley, Leslie J. Francis, and Colin Crowder (Leominster, U.K.: Gracewing, 1996), 106.

32. Dykstra, "No Longer Strangers," 109; cf. 110 and 113. "Our faith as individuals (and even as particular congregations and denominations) is our participation in the redemptive activity of God by the power of the Spirit through the church." That Dykstra considers mission to be defined in the same terms was confirmed through a phone interview. The church's mission is, broadly conceived, her participation in the ongoing redemptive activity of God. In the interview, he stated, "The church is defined by participation in the redemptive activity of God." Additionally, in the transcripts are the following notes: "Mission is — [and he filled in the blank] 'participation in the ongoing redemptive activity of God in the world.' I pointed out that what he called 'contemporary developments in Reformed theology' (i.e. Moltmann, Barth and C67) is really the beginning of a more self-aware missional theology. He agreed. I said that the very marks of the Church were being called into question and he vigorously agreed." Excerpts from my notes based on a phone interview, April 26, 2007.

33. Dykstra, "No Longer Strangers," 109.

34. Dykstra, "No Longer Strangers," 109.

Christian faith "involves active engagement in certain practices which are central to and constitutive of the church's life."[35] These practices are ways in which individuals open themselves to the redemptive activity of God and participate in that activity.

Dykstra's definition of church, like his conception of Christian practices, continues to build in significant ways upon Edward Farley's notion of *ecclesia* as developed in *Ecclesial Man*. Farley's aim in *Ecclesial Man* is to address head-on the loss of confidence and nerve in theology. He explains, "In recent years the theological community had entertained what might be called a nasty suspicion about itself." This suspicion is that there is no "reality" behind the language of faith and that Christian theologians are stockbrokers who distribute stock in a nonexistent company.[36] Faith, then, has no unique or distinguishing content and apprehends no reality. That Farley is interested in dealing with this reality is emphatically announced by his use of the word "reality" or "realities" language 111 times in the first twenty-one pages of his book! It is this "reality" that he wishes to uncover before the uncertain Christian. This reality is, according to Farley, the reality of God, Jesus Christ, creation, end-time, and salvation.[37] Farley concludes, drawing on Edmund Husserl's studies in phenomenology and on his own phenomenological theology,[38] that the apprehension of these realities by faith is inextricably bound to a community that is marked by a redemptive alteration of existence, a language that accommodates that modification, and a faith world or social matrix that supports a determinate intersubjectivity.

Of particular importance for Dykstra is Farley's description of *ecclesia* as a unique form of corporate historical existence and his explanation of its role in "mediating distinctive realities."[39] What Farley highlights, and this is picked up and developed by Dykstra, are the conditions under which "faith's apprehensions" may be possible. He suggests that these conditions include, at their core, a specific form of redemptive human corporate historical existence, or *ecclesia* that is characterized by a redemptive modification of corporate existence.[40] The actual apprehension of

35. Dykstra, "No Longer Strangers," 114.

36. Farley, *Ecclesial Man*, 6.

37. Farley, *Ecclesial Man*, 17.

38. Phenomenological theology is "the attempt to penetrate and describe the prereflective matrix of faith's acts and structures." Farley, *Ecclesial Man*, 51.

39. Farley, *Ecclesial Man*, xiv.

40. Farley, *Ecclesial Man*, 21.

"reality" occurs by participation in this community and, as Dykstra later adds, the practices that constitute the church's life.

While Dykstra never uses Farley's phenomenological language himself, one can clearly discern in Dykstra's writings on the church language that has its origin in Farley's discussion of *ecclesia*. The following themes from Farley can be discerned in Dykstra's ecclesiology: the governing definition of the church in terms of apprehending redemption; the notion of the community rendering a faith world; the idea that connected to this faith world is a God, often encountered as a preconscious normative and determinate intersubjectivity that reshapes human consciousness toward redemptive existence; the idea that the reality and presence of God is, in an essential way, socially mediated; and the idea that the redemptive mode of existence intrinsically involves freedom for and obligation to those who remain outside the orbit of *ecclesia*. There is always a referent beyond the provincial expressions of church.[41] *Ecclesia* has a "peculiar way of referring beyond itself and its own faith-world to the stranger, the strange other."[42] All the aforementioned aspects of Dykstra's ecclesiology that are taken from Farley's work are then passed through the prism of Reformed theology so that they speak more directly about divine agency and are related to the ongoing redemptive work of God.

Practices, Ecclesiology, and the Ministry of the Congregation

The context in which Dykstra has unfolded his theory of Christian practices has been in the service of the educational ministry of the church. What, then, is Christian education? And how do the practices support this ministry? In his words, "Christian education is that particular work which

41. Despite his heavy dependence on Schleiermacher, upon whose theology no missiologist has built a case for the missional church, Farley offers some building material for a church defined by its mission. For example, in his essential *Theologia*, Farley advances the idea that the Christian community is defined by its nature as a redemptive community and then continues to state, "the education of a leadership for a redemptive community cannot be *defined* by reference to the public tasks and acts by which the community endures (a formal approach), but rather by the requirements set by the nature of that community as redemptive." Edward Farley, *Theologia: The Fragmentation and Unity of Theological Education* (Philadelphia: Fortress, 1983), 127-28.

42. Farley, *Ecclesial Man*, 165.

the church does to teach the historical, communal, difficult and counter-cultural practices of the church so that the church may learn to participate in them ever more fully and deeply."[43] So education for this dynamic church, which is defined by its participation in the redemptive activity of God, is a practice-centered ministry, marked by initiation into and deepening participation in formative Christian practices.

If the church is defined in terms of its mission or co-mission in the world, then the practices and initiation into the practices (discipleship) should bear the mark of God's redemptive and dynamic presence. In fact, in one of his earliest published essays, in response to Albert Winn's thematic study of the Gospel of John entitled *A Sense of Mission*,[44] Dykstra concludes, "If we want to know who the church is, we must see it not as the people who know God best, who love God most, or who have God's greatest blessing but as the 'sent people' of God — people sent by God through Jesus Christ."[45] In his own application of the insights offered by Winn, as it relates to Christian education, Dykstra asserts: "Now, I want to make two claims about Christian education and nurture. First, all Christian nurture and education are for the sake of mission. That's why we do it. That's its purpose. Second, nurture and education are themselves forms of mission."[46] Is it possible that this commitment to mission is never abandoned by Dykstra but is in fact pervasive in his thought if not always explicit? Certainly, Dykstra could have followed Winn to articulate a more nuanced understanding of mission or of the Christian as sent. Winn, drawing upon Barth, concludes, "the experience that makes a person a Christian is the experience in which Christ sends that person, gives that person a mission."[47] He continues to explain that the popular ideas that a Christian is one who lives by a certain moral code or a Christian is one who has received grace and enjoys the benefits of salvation only make sense in light of our commission.[48]

I have attempted to coax out the missional aspect of his work to demonstrate how there is, latent in Dykstra's work, an interest in the mission

43. Dykstra, "No Longer Strangers," 117.
44. Winn, *A Sense of Mission*.
45. Dykstra, *Growing in the Life of Faith*, 158.
46. Dykstra, *Growing in the Life of Faith*, 159.
47. Winn, *A Sense of Mission*, 62.
48. See my treatment of Barth's understanding of the Christian as witness, 34-39, above.

of the church. I have also argued that he exhibits a willingness to consider and appropriate missional theology. That Dykstra made such an assertion so specifically and firmly early in his career that "all Christian nurture and education are for the sake of mission" evokes the question, why did this graphic sense of mission not play a central or determinative role in the ways he wrote about practices and guided the discussion in the following years?

Among recent works to take the challenge of missional theology seriously, "Foundations for Missional Christian Education," the doctoral dissertation of Claire A. Smith, draws heavily on the work of Guder, the Gospel and Our Culture Network (GOCN), and Letty Russell[49] to make the point that "[i]n the various approaches to Christian education that are widely followed, *none takes as its starting point and foundation an understanding of the church as missionary by its very nature.*"[50] Smith, while offering insight into the necessary connection between mission and Christian education/ formation, never addresses the issue of practical theology's emphasis on Christian practices as God's means for strengthening and sustaining Christian identity and promoting a way of life that is good. She, accordingly, offers only glancing attention to the important work of Dykstra. Smith, following John L. Elias,[51] characterizes Dykstra, along with Fowler, as being among the "faith development" approaches to Christian education.

Smith argues, correctly, that none of the contemporary approaches to Christian education build upon the foundational understanding of the missionary nature of the church.[52] She claims that while Dykstra identifies mission as the purpose of Christian education, in his *Growing in the Life of Faith* he deals with mission as a "postscript rather than as central to his work."[53] Smith is correct in that what Dykstra does fail to do is explicitly

49. Participant of the North American Working Group of the Missionary Structure of the Congregation study of the Department on Studies in Evangelism of the World Council of Churches, who later applied insights garnered from her participation in that study to the study of Christian education.

50. Claire Annelise Smith, "Foundations for Missional Christian Education" (Ph.D. diss., Union Theological Seminary and Presbyterian School of Christian Education, 2005), 2, emphasis in original.

51. John L. Elias, *A History of Christian Education: Protestant, Catholic, and Orthodox Perspectives* (Malabar, Fla.: Krieger, 2002).

52. Smith, "Foundations," 9-10.

53. Smith, "Foundations," 11-12.

name the ongoing redemptive work of God as mission and connect God's mission intentionally to the being and purpose of the church. Having worked through Dykstra's writings and personally corresponded with him, I believe once one understands Dykstra's way of speaking about mission in terms of participation in the ongoing redemptive work of God, the idea of mission can be found embedded in virtually every other essay in that collection. I do not, however, argue with Smith's conclusion given how little explicit attention Dykstra has given to the issue of mission. Most of his essays are set within the conversation about faith formation, and "participation" in those discussions tends to mean becoming aware of, recognizing, and finally sharing in all that the creative and redemptive activity of God extends to and provides people. There is no sense, yet, that in Dykstra's writings or in the *Practicing Our Faith* discussion that "participation in the ongoing redemptive work of God" is suggesting, as missional theology would insist, that the congregation become the active, sent agents who are the sign, instrument, and foretaste of the kingdom of God. The latent theological accents that I have highlighted above suggest that this gap is not unbridgeable.

Conclusion

Craig Dykstra and the *Practicing Our Faith* conversation have initiated a discussion about the Christian faith that has important consequences for theological education, Christian discipleship, and congregational life. Among the important contributions of the practices conversation is the idea that the practices help us to perform a way of life in the world that is faithful to God's intentions. The practices put us in a position to perceive the mysteries of God, focus on participation in Christ, and provide the arena in which knowledge of God is tested and palpably felt.[54] God changes his people as they participate in Christian practices. Through these practices we are no longer strangers to God's redemptive presence in the world. Christian witness is the result of a Christian life together that is nurtured by these practices.

---

54. Dykstra believes that Christian practices are "constitutive of the kind of community life through which God's presence is palpably felt and known." Dykstra, *Growing in the Life of Faith*, 53.

The question of the next chapter is, how would these important insights of the practices discussion be altered if the missional latency that I find in Dykstra's work were drawn out? If, as Dykstra has suggested, faith is "appropriate and intentional participation in the redemptive activity of God," then how should such faith shape our understanding of Christian practices? If, as Dykstra has suggested, mission is the purpose of Christian education and Christian education is mission, what does that say about the practices that constitute the curriculum? How would we perceive practices differently if mission were not thought of as the overflow or result of the practices but were, instead, the first thought that shaped the list of practices? The remainder of the book will address these issues.

CHAPTER FIVE

Practicing Witness

How might the missional theology coming out of the *Missional Church* conversation alter the definition or conception of Christian practices offered by Valparaiso? As Bass and Dykstra have explained, "Christian practices are things Christian people do together over time in response to and in light of God's active presence for the life of the world [in Jesus Christ]."[1] In this chapter, I will address the enduring value of the practices discussion for missional theology, and I will consider how a missional theological starting point reorients the *Practicing Our Faith* definition of Christian practices given above. Then I will reengage Serene Jones's essay from *Practicing Theology* and explain how the missional perspective can contribute to her important insights about how central doctrines of the Reformed faith offer a distinctive orientation to Christian practices. Having addressed the *Practicing Our Faith* approach to Christian practices, I will then return to Dykstra's particular contribution to a theology of Christian practices and consider how practices are both formative and performative, how they address both worship and witness, how practicing our faith is really practicing our witness. Then, since, according to the practices discussion, worship is the master practice, I will briefly explore the relationship between worship and mission and argue that mission is not an optional second movement for the worshiping community. I will conclude with some

1. Dorothy C. Bass, ed., *Practicing Our Faith: A Way of Life for a Searching People* (San Francisco: Jossey-Bass, 1997), 5.

thoughts about an extended conversation between missional theology and the practices discussion about Christian discipleship.

The Enduring Importance of the Practices Discussion for Missional Theology

The definition and six aspects of Christian practices that I highlighted in the third chapter, as well as the application of the Valparaiso theory of practices in the books associated with it, could lend some shape and direction to the missional church discussion of practices. How can the performances, patterns, and ways of witness described in the theology of the *Missional Church* discussion be given further form by considering the historical, social, universal, local, and conversional/transformational aspects of practices highlighted by the *Practicing Our Faith* conversation? To date, the rich body of literature associated with the Valparaiso Project has not been sufficiently attended to. But beyond the benefits of adding some shape to an important conversation in missional theology, Dykstra's practices way of thinking about discipleship and faith formation could help missional theologians to consider how a missional congregation is cultivated. The space that Dykstra claims practices create is the space in which the gospel-church-culture encounter transforms our understanding of what it means to call Jesus Lord, because the encounter occurs in the practice of the faith and in a specific place and time. It is the space that is necessary for the cultural pluriformity of the gospel to find expression. It is the space in which our witness is strengthened as our knowledge of God is tested, confirmed, and palpably felt.[2] It is the space where we realize that we are a called people of God who are no longer strangers to God's redemptive presence in the world. It is the space where our identity as Christians is formed and nurtured. All this is essential to the missional church.

Furthermore, the practices way of talking about discipleship can ground a conversation that has been accused of being primarily an abstract, technical, and academic discussion that seems removed from the

---

2. Instead of "palpably felt," perhaps Calvin would say our knowledge of God is "sealed upon our hearts through the Holy Spirit." John Calvin, *Institutes of the Christian Religion*, ed. John T. McNeill, trans. Ford Lewis Battles, Library of Christian Classics, vols. 20-21 (Philadelphia: Westminster, 1960), 551.

practical life of congregations.³ The ministry of the congregation, which responds to the mission of God and shares in the prophetic role of Jesus Christ by the Spirit, is to bear witness to the reality of the kingdom of God. Yet this witness is played out in the pedestrian activities that constitute our living and are performed by finite creatures of time, who "need speech that is truthful, decisions that are well-considered, and communities that are structured to permit the just and full participation of all."⁴ The practices literature engages these basic human conditions. Together, practical theology and missional theology can promote a notion of practice-centered discipleship that accounts for the witness of the church and at the same time recognizes that the reign of God also includes the "habitations of the Spirit"⁵ that we share in now as we participate in God's redemptive activity in the world. This is discipleship, and this is what the practices conversation and what missional theology are really about. Michael Warren rightly understood the potential impact of the *Practicing Our Faith* series when he opined, "My suspicion is that time may show that book [*Practicing Our Faith*] to be a breakthrough in conceptualizing the specifics of discipleship."⁶

Warren's observation has been confirmed with the recent release of the next book in the series, *For Life Abundant: Practical Theology, Theological Education, and Christian Ministry,* and especially in Kathleen Cahalan's contribution with James Nieman, "Mapping the Field of Practical Theol-

3. Alan Roxburgh, who has been invested in the missional church conversation since the beginning, recognizes the critique in Alan Roxburgh, "The Missional Church," *Theology Matters: A Publication of Presbyterians for Faith, Family and Ministry* 10, no. 4 (September/October 2004): 4-5. See also Alan J. Roxburgh and M. Scott Boren, *Introducing the Missional Church: What It Is, Why It Matters, How to Become One* (Grand Rapids: Baker, 2009), 10.

4. Dorothy C. Bass, preface to *Practicing Our Faith,* xii.

5. The term "habitations of the Spirit" is taken from Dykstra. He explains it in the following way: "I described the practices of the Christian faith as habitations of the Spirit. They are not, finally, activities we do to make something spiritual happen in our lives. Nor are they duties we undertake to be obedient to God. Rather, they are patterns of communal action that create openings in our lives where the grace, mercy, and presence of God may be made known to us. They are places where the power of God is experienced. In the end, these are not ultimately our practices but forms of participation in the practice of God." Craig R. Dykstra, *Growing in the Life of Faith: Education and Christian Practices* (Louisville: Westminster John Knox, 2005), 66. See also xv, 64, and 78.

6. Michael Warren's editorial notes in Dorothy C. Bass and Craig R. Dykstra, "Christian Practices and Congregational Education in Faith," in *Changing Churches: The Local Church and the Structures of Change,* ed. Michael Warren (Portland, Oreg.: Pastoral Press, 2000), 247.

ogy." Cahalan and Nieman suggest that promoting, supporting, and sustaining "lived discipleship" is the unifying purpose that orients practical theology.[7] Furthermore, and important to bringing together missional theology and practical theology, is the authors' claim that a theological mandate is attached to Christian discipleship such that "Communities of disciples do not exist for their own sake. Wherever they live, disciples instead seek what will enable their richer service of and witness before others."[8] This discipleship is, as the missional theologians insist, an apostolic discipleship that unites action and reflection with the goal of making our witness more "faithful and effective."[9] With the release of *For Life Abundant,* and drawing on the resource of Craig Dykstra's theology of practices, the stage has been set for an important interdisciplinary dialogue between missiology and practical theology about Christian practices and the church's witness that will extend well beyond the conclusions of this book.

As a collegial interchange, missional theology could add some important insights and depth to the six aspects of Christian practices explained in chapter 3. For example, on the historical aspect of Christian practices, the *Practicing Our Faith* conversation suggests that the practices may be "significantly" reshaped, "reformed and transformed." The application of missional theology's gospel-culture-church triad and multicultural perspective may reveal that many of our practices have a perpetuity and constancy that, having followed the pattern of Christendom and developed with a Western perspective, makes them resistant to any substantial alteration.

For example, on the social nature of practices, Bass and Dykstra suggest, "Christian practices appear in slightly different forms in each unique local congregation and surrounding community."[10] If one were to incorporate the inculturation dimension of missional theology into the practices discussion, one would have to consider the fact that the practice of healing in sub-Saharan Africa, for example, outside of Lilongwe, Malawi, is significantly different from the practice of healing in a Presbyterian

7. Kathleen A. Cahalan and James R. Nieman, "Mapping the Field of Practical Theology," in *For Life Abundant: Practical Theology, Theological Education, and Christian Ministry,* ed. Dorothy C. Bass and Craig R. Dykstra (Grand Rapids: Eerdmans, 2008), 67.

8. Cahalan and Nieman, "Mapping the Field," 68.

9. Cahalan and Nieman, "Mapping the Field," 69.

10. Bass and Dykstra, "Christian Practices," 260.

church in Williamsburg, Virginia. While both address issues of illness, frailty, and finitude, the church in Malawi does so in a context that includes ancestral spirits, witch doctors, and superstition.[11] Furthermore, in Malawi the practice of healing is conducted in a culture that largely rejects the individualistic and competitive perspective of contemporary Western culture and embraces the connectedness of humanity. What could such a cross-cultural perspective reveal about the holistic nature of the practice of healing?

Building on Edward Farley's "principle of positivity,"[12] and resonant from the missional theology of mission scholar Lamin Sanneh, it is possible to conclude that authentic Christian practices relativize any one expression of a Christian practice and destigmatize any other possible local expressions, freeing practices to make use of all indigenous resources and agency to forge an authentically Christian practice that is appropriate to a particular setting.[13] Missional theology will challenge the practices discussion to engage robustly this ecumenical and intercultural perspective. As Hastings has suggested about practical theology in general, the practices conversation could also benefit from missiology's ecumenical insights into the way in which witness is practiced in all its cultural diversity and its multiformity of expressions worldwide. This ecumenical vision could serve as a means of critiquing local practices that become normative or stagnant, having lost any sense of tension within their own cultural environs.[14]

---

11. Janet L. Brown, "HIV/AIDS Alienation: Between Prejudice and Acceptance" (University of Stellenbosch, 2004).

12. Farley argues in *Ecclesial Man*, as summarized by Don Richter, that the Christian faith "both requires yet relativizes its cultural embodiments." See Edward Farley, *Ecclesial Man: A Social Phenomenology of Faith and Reality* (Philadelphia: Fortress, 1975), 57-64, where he explains his principle of positivity. Also, see Don Carl Richter's engagement and appropriation of Farley in his dissertation, "Christian Nurture in Congregations: Ecclesial Practices as Social Means of Grace" (Ph.D. diss., Princeton Theological Seminary, 1992), 259-320.

13. Sanneh promotes the thesis in *Translating the Message* that Christianity from it origins is a religion that expands by means of translation. In the beginning that meant relativizing yet promoting certain aspects of its Jewish heritage and destigmatizing and adopting certain aspects of Gentile culture. This process does and must continue due to the very nature of the gospel. Lamin O. Sanneh, *Translating the Message: The Missionary Impact on Culture*, American Society of Missiology Series, no. 13 (Maryknoll, N.Y.: Orbis, 1989).

14. Thomas John Hastings, *Practical Theology and the One Body of Christ: Toward a Missional-Ecumenical Model*, Studies in Practical Theology (Grand Rapids: Eerdmans, 2007). See my summary of Hastings's thesis in chapter 3.

One important insight of the practices conversation has to do with how the practices function to communicate knowledge of God. Missional theology emphasizes that the practices do not only bear epistemological weight, but they also offer a kind of knowledge of God available only through participation in God's reconciling activity in the world. The union with Christ that is the goal of Christian practices is a dynamic union in mission; a sharing in the prophetic activity of Christ. Therefore, true Christian practices bear a kind of evangelistic weight; they are the means by which the community embodies its witness to the reality of the reign and rule of God.[15] With respect to the social aspect of Christian practices, and how the impact of practices spills over into the world, missional theology insists that mission cannot be understood as a by-product or effect of something called "faith formation." Mission is not an "add-on" to Christian life or beneficial outcome of it; mission is essential to it.

This leads us to consider, finally, the impact that missional theology could have on the witnessing aspect of Christian practices. Newbigin's understanding of the missionary church as a sign, instrument, and foretaste of the kingdom of God might serve as a helpful ground-level entry into dialogue between missional theology and Valparaiso about Christian practices.[16] Accepting that the church is embodied by the practices of the faith,

15. That is, to the degree that one's notion of evangelism is not attenuated and is set within its proper context of witness. For more on evangelism as "incarnational witness," see Darrell L. Guder, *The Incarnation and the Church's Witness*, Christian Mission and Modern Culture (Harrisburg, Pa.: Trinity, 1999). William Abraham defines evangelism as "primary initiation into the kingdom of God" and argues that in the early church "one could be relatively sure that the verbal proclamation of the gospel would be intimately linked to the Christian community and to the other ministries of the church that are essential to the rebirth and growth of the new believer." William J. Abraham, *The Logic of Evangelism* (Grand Rapids: Eerdmans, 1989), 13 and 57, respectively. Guder's understanding of evangelism is rooted in the *missio Dei*, shaped in its method, content, and strategy by the life of Jesus Christ, and is the heart of the ministry of the church. In agreement with Bosch, Guder characterizes evangelism as consisting in "the proclamation of salvation in Christ to nonbelievers, in announcing forgiveness of sins, in calling people to repentance and faith in Christ, inviting them to become living members of Christ's earthly community and to begin a life in the power of the Holy Spirit." Darrell L. Guder, *The Continuing Conversion of the Church*, Gospel and Our Culture Series (Grand Rapids: Eerdmans, 2000), 25-26.

16. This triad, of sign, instrument, and foretaste, which became a common way for Newbigin to describe the church, was employed by Newbigin in one of its earliest forms in J. E. Lesslie Newbigin, *The Household of God: Lectures on the Nature of the Church* (London: SCM, 1953).

one could conclude, in the words of Newbigin, "They are to be a *sign*, pointing men to something that is beyond their present horizon but can give guidance and hope now; an *instrument* (not the only one) that God can use for his work of healing, liberating and blessing; and a *firstfruit* [*foretaste*] — a place where men and women can have a real taste now of the joy and freedom God intends for all."[17] Perhaps the practices, like the church they instantiate, could be understood in these terms.

The practices are signs of the kingdom — they are not themselves the kingdom and do not usher it in, but they do point beyond themselves to the living Lord Jesus who is the one sign of the kingdom. The practices are instruments but are not merely instrumental. While at times speaking of the church in terms of its commission can seem to present the church as merely instrumental to mission, Newbigin challenged what he felt were the instrumental and functional views of the church.[18] Following Newbigin's logic, the practices can be considered places where encounter happens, and they can be a "means of grace," though grace cannot be manipulated through the practices. Finally, the practices offer a foretaste of the kingdom. The suspicion that Farley spoke of, that there is really no reality behind all the rhetoric of religion, melts away when one encounters the palpable reality of the risen Christ through receiving or extending hospitality, or experiences the restoration of communion that accompanies the extending or receiving of forgiveness. The practices always serve the ministry of the church and the mission of the God.

17. J. E. Lesslie Newbigin, *A Word in Season: Perspectives on Christian World Missions* (Grand Rapids: Eerdmans, 1994), 33.

18. His challenge to Hoekendijk appears in Newbigin, *The Household of God*, 148. Of Mackay, Newbigin adds, in reviewing MacKay's *Ecumenics*, "One can agree that the Church is not an end in itself, and yet be uncomfortable with the purely functional account of the Church which some passages in the present volume suggest. God does not love men as a means to an end; he loves them! This surely means that the debate as to whether the Church is a means or an end is barren. The Church is neither: it is the first-fruit of God's redeeming action, and is therefore the place where God's love is known as a reality, a reality which impels us to share it." J. E. Lesslie Newbigin, "Ecumenics: The Science of the Church Universal," *Princeton Seminary Bulletin* 59 (1965): 61.

Christian Practices from the Perspective of Missional Theology

We have examined the following definition of Christian practices:

> Christian practices are things Christian people do together over time in response to and in light of God's active presence for the life of the world [in Jesus Christ].

If we approach the task of expressing our understanding of Christian practices from the perspective of missional theology, then that definition could be replaced with this one: *Christian practices are the Spirit-filled and embodied signs, instruments, and foretastes of the kingdom of God that Christian people participate in together over time to partake in, partner with, and witness to God's redemptive presence for the life of the world in Jesus Christ.*

Revisiting Serene Jones's Graced Practices

As I have already affirmed, Serene Jones made important observations about how the Reformed doctrine of justification highlights the freedom we have in selecting and shaping our practices and about how the doctrine of sanctification challenges us to execute our practices in a way that is excellent. Given what has been said about the missionary nature of the church, we now need to answer the question, what distinctive orientation toward the practices does the doctrine of vocation give to the practices? What difference should it make that Christian practices issue from and embody a church that is, following the nature of God, missionary by its very nature? My answer, which should be self-evident by this point, is that the doctrine of vocation emphasizes the witnessing aspect of the practices. When a community or an individual participates in the practices of the Christian faith, he or she is *practicing witness*. To Jones's formulae of "freedom for practices" and "excellence in practices," I add the next, and essential, step of *witness through practices*. With the doctrine of vocation in view, the practices can be understood to be forming (sanctification), freed (justification), and proclamatory (vocation).[19]

19. Serene Jones, "Graced Practices: Excellence and Freedom in the Christian Life," in *Practicing Theology: Beliefs and Practices in Christian Life*, ed. Miroslav Volf and Dorothy C. Bass (Grand Rapids: Eerdmans, 2002), 72. Proclamatory here should be understood in terms of

Karl Barth has drawn attention to the fact that the self-revelation of God reveals a God who, in Jesus Christ, has always existed for humanity. The act and being of God are related such that God's missionary movement toward the world is not a secondary or extra move — "God is a missionary God."[20] In a similar manner, the church is the apostolic community that corresponds to the ongoing prophetic activity of Jesus, and it cannot be defined apart from its world-relatedness. Barth could challenge us to consider how the practices relate to the witnessing ministry of the church — in what ways do Christian practices correspond to the ongoing prophetic activity of Jesus Christ? The role of "witness" or "minister" does not belong to a special class of Christian; it is received at baptism and is what makes one a Christian.

The question of vocation is latent in Jones's essay and can be lifted out by attending to such phrases as "in their function as witness" and "contextual appropriateness of its witness" and questions like, "What is the culture of the city in which our practices are performed as witness?"[21] Though the term "witness" is present in these phrases, the undergirding theological material of a missional theology is not there to support it. Missional theology helps to develop such themes and give these questions a more prominent place in the discussion about Christian practices — the beginning place. *Questions about the witnessing aspect of the practices are questions that relate to the very nature and purpose of the church and are the reason why the questions of freedom for and excellence in practices are so vital.*

Darrell Guder, building upon the insights of early missional theologians, drawing on a missional theological interpretation of Barth, and employing a missional hermeneutic of Scripture,[22] has helped us to under-

---

Barth's insistence that, in the specific forms of witness of the witnessing community, "its speech is also action and its action speech." Karl Barth, *The Doctrine of Reconciliation*, vol. IV/3.2 of *Church Dogmatics*, ed. G. W. Bromiley and T. F. Torrance (Edinburgh: T. & T. Clark, 1962), 862-63.

20. The title of John Flett's dissertation in which he makes that case by drawing on Barth's theology; John Graeme Flett, "God Is a Missionary God: Missio Dei, Karl Barth, and the Doctrine of the Trinity" (Ph.D. diss., Princeton Theological Seminary, 2007).

21. Jones, "Graced Practices," 67.

22. Following Bosch, Guder has embraced a missional hermeneutic, defined in the following way: reading the Scripture in such a way that its central emphasis upon forming the community of disciples for mission is emphasized. Darrell L. Guder, "Biblical Formation and Discipleship," in *Treasure in Clay Jars: Patterns in Missional Faithfulness*, ed. Lois Barrett et al. (Grand Rapids: Eerdmans, 2004), 60-61.

stand that the important Reformed doctrines of justification and sanctification must be expressed through vocation or witness.

Revisiting Craig Dykstra's Theology of Christian Practices

Craig Dykstra, while drawing on the insights of early missional theologians, does not yet advance the practices discussion to what one could consider missionally informed practices. The progenitors of missional theology that Dykstra quotes emphasize that the church is defined by her sent-ness; that discipleship is discipleship in the execution of a task, witness; and that the marks of the church, as they have been traditionally conceived, do not adequately address that which is most essential to her nature — her vocation. These Reformed theologians were challenging the very definition of the church, and Dykstra, by reference to them, was connecting his discussion of the disciplines and practices of the Christian faith to a church that is, according to these theologians, defined in terms of her mission. In a missional vision of Christian practices, the practices are always connected both to God's redemptive activity in the world and to his community to which is given the ministry of reconciliation. Christian practices instantiate the church that exists in service to and in partnership with God's redemptive activity. It follows, though Dykstra does not make the connection directly, that the practices that constitute the outward life of the redemptive and witnessing community must be marked by an emerging missional quality.

While Dykstra references the progenitors of missional theology, he never seriously engages what the issues they raise would or should imply about the topics he addresses. To the degree that the practices are Christian practices, they reflect the Trinitarian God who births them and sustains them; they constitute the way of life of a missional church and are oriented to God's ongoing work in the world.

These practices are ways in which individuals open themselves to the redemptive activity of God and participate in that activity. In other words, to consider Dykstra's potential contribution to the theology of Christian practices, from the perspective of missional theology, participation in the practices is the way in which the congregation is prepared for and engages in mission. Participating in Christian practices is how we live out our Christian discipleship, which is an apostolic discipleship. The practices that, in Dykstra's estimation, constitute the Christian educational curriculum of the church and prepare the people for ministry are expressive and formative of a community defined by its commission to follow God in God's ongoing redemptive mission in the world.

In the interest of affirming the value of Dykstra's most significant contributions to the practices way of thinking about discipleship, and with the goal of presenting the missional interpretation of Christian practices, I will restate my questions for Dykstra's theology of Christian practices.

How would the important insights of the practices discussion be altered if the missional latency that I find in Dykstra's work were accented? If, as Dykstra has suggested, faith is "appropriate and intentional participation in the redemptive activity of God," then how should such faith shape our understanding of Christian practices? If, as Dykstra has suggested, mission is the purpose of Christian education and Christian education is mission, what does that say about the practices that constitute the curriculum? How would we perceive practices differently if mission were not thought of as the overflow or result of the practices but were, instead, the first thought that shaped the list of practices? Below I will show how the formative value of practicing one's faith is transformed by a missional perspective into the performative witness of practicing witness.

Dykstra's language and approach to practicing the Christian faith emphasize the idea that the practices help us to live a way of life in the world that is faithful to God's intentions. The consistent application of missional theological insights would in no way diminish this important contribution, but would emphasize the idea that Christian practices help us to see that this way of life is the performance of a way of witness to the kingdom of God in the world. Dykstra emphasizes that Christian practices put us in a position to perceive the mysteries of God. Missional theology adds that Christian practices are the way in which we bear witness to those mysteries in the world. Dykstra emphasizes that the practices focus on participation in Christ and provide the arena in which knowledge of God is tested and palpably felt — they create a space where God works in us. Missionally conceived, Christian practices are signs, instruments, and foretastes of the kingdom of God and are the way in which an active working fellowship with Christ is lived — they create a space where God, through the Holy Spirit, works through us. Dykstra demonstrates theologically how through these practices we are no longer strangers to God's redemptive presence in the world. The missional accent, which in no way depreciates Dykstra's contribution, is that through Christian practices we proclaim and perform God's redemptive presence for the world. Finally, according to the *Practicing Our Faith* conversation, Christian witness is the result of a Christian life together that is nurtured by these practices. For the missional theologian witness is the purpose of the Christian life together that is cultivated through practices.

By viewing the Valparaiso conversation about the practices of the Christian faith with a missional lens, I find a theological vision for discipleship that I term "practicing witness." From Christian practices in which great formative value inheres, I draw out the performative value that helps us to understand them as signs, foretastes, and instruments of God's kingdom. The chart on page 99, as with most simplifications, borders on a caricature of both the *Practicing Our Faith* and *Practicing Witness* conceptions of Christian practices. Nonetheless, I believe it is accurate in representing both the importance and the limitations of the contemporary practices discussion. It should be understood that I am not suggesting that one side replace the other; practicing our faith is practicing witness. The two lists are not intended to stand over and against one another with the "Practicing Witness" list replacing the "Practicing Our Faith" catalogue. Neither does the conjunction "and" adequately explain the relationship between the two understandings of Christian practices. While the two approaches are both complementary and interactive, the missional approach to practices necessarily influences our understanding of Christian practices at a fundamental level. The missional perspective enriches the current practices conversation and reorients the whole discussion about Christian practices toward the missional vocation of the church. The Christian way of life in the world is the way of witness. If it is true that there is no participation in Christ that does not include partnership in his mission in the world, then the missional perspective is not an optional additive. How the missional perspective should influence the practices way of thinking about discipleship is clearly revealed in the last pairing ("worship as the master practice" and "witness as the master practice"), as I will explain below.

Practicing Our Faith		Practicing Witness
A way of life in the world.		A way of witness to the kingdom of God in the world.
The practices put us in a position to perceive mysteries of God.		Through practices we proclaim and perform (witness) God's redemptive presence for the world.
Participation in Christ — practices are the arena where knowledge of God is tested and palpably felt.		Partnership with Christ — practices are a sign, instrument, and foretaste of the kingdom of God and are the way in which an active working fellowship with Christ is lived.
Practices create space where God works in us.	AND	Practices create space where God works through us.
God changes his people as they participate in practices.		God changes the world through the witness of the practices.
Through the practices we are "no longer strangers to God's redemptive presence in the world."		The practices enable us to bear witness to those mysteries in the world.
Witness is the result of the Christian life together that is nurtured by practices.		Witness is the purpose of the Christian life together that is cultivated through practices.
Emphasizes worship as the master practice.		Emphasizes witness as the master practice.

Missio Dei, Worship, and Witness

In the *Practicing Our Faith* discussion, worship is regarded as the master practice. I believe that worship is a master practice of the church. As I explained in chapter 2, in Barth's missional theology the church "gathered" and "scattered," as it is often perceived, cannot be properly understood if there is a tension or contrast set up between the cult or liturgical worship and the mission of the church. Both are comprehended by the *missio Dei.* There is no such thing as true worship that is not missional, just as there is no such thing as true mission that is not worship. Barth's conviction is that the connection between liturgy and mission is made manifest in baptism, the liturgical entry point into Christian discipleship. Baptism is an ordination to ministry and a call to participate in the ongoing mission of the living Christ through witness. Equally, missional theology considers the kerygmatic aspects of baptism and the Lord's Supper as proclamations of that which is and is to come — a witness to the *missio Dei*. From the side of liturgical theology this point is made especially well by Gordon Lathrop, who claims that "the gifts at the heart of worship all turn inside out."[23] The points we strain to make today about the connection between worship and mission are natural in the New Testament, which consistently employs cultic language to describe the ongoing mission and ministry of the Christian community.[24]

While ignoring the relationship between worship and mission signals a significant theological deficiency, considering the liturgical or formal worship service of the church in utilitarian terms as merely a preparation for mission is equally ill conceived. While more has been written recently on the relationship between worship and mission, one of the enduring monographs was written by J. G. Davies, who wrote his work in response to his own participation in the European Working Group of the Missionary Structure of the Congregation project of the World Council of Churches.[25] Davies is an important early voice in a growing missional imagination about worship. Davies' comments are particularly germane to this brief exploration of worship and will help to properly locate the practices discussion in the worship of the church.

> If we think in terms of utility, then worship becomes the occasion of gathering preparatory to sending. Worship provides a source of power to enable Christians to engage in another activity outside the cultic act. Worship, it may be said, strengthens us for mission, the two being related as cause and effect. Against this it has to be affirmed that worship

23. Gordon W. Lathrop, "Liturgy and Mission in the North American Context," in *Inside Out: Worship in an Age of Mission*, ed. Thomas H. Schattauer (Minneapolis: Fortress, 1999), 202.

24. To mention a few, consider the offering of the community's life as a "living sacrifice" (Rom. 12:1-2); the ministry of Paul to the Philippians as a drink offering and their faith as a sacrifice (Phil. 2:17-18); the characterization of Christ's own work in fulfilling his mission as "a fragrant offering and sacrifice" (Eph. 5:2); or Paul's description of his ministry in Macedonia in similar terms (2 Cor. 2:14-16).

25. In one recent work on the relationship between worship and mission, Thomas Schattauer finds in Davies' approach the model for his "inside out" or "radically traditional" approach that becomes the overarching theme of the entire work. See Schattauer, *Inside Out*.

is not a means to mission; it is one facet of the divine activity which also includes mission. We do not therefore prepare for mission by worshipping, although we should be missionary in our worship. The cultus is not an isolated activity but part of the totality of the divine movement through Christ and by the Spirit in which worship and mission are united. The same idea may be given alternate expression in the form that worship has not an evangelizing function per se since all evangelization undertaken to the glory of God is worship. Indeed, once we realize that mission is *missio Dei*, then we can appreciate that worship too is part of God's mission.[26]

This missional approach to worship is crucial for properly locating the practices discussion. It avoids possible contested boundaries between the inner and outer life of the congregation by comprehending both within the mission of God. Frank Senn claimed to pick up Davies' concern but modify it to "indicate ways in which worship is itself an aspect of the mission of God."[27] Senn's sacramental approach advances Davies' argument about the relationship between worship and mission by considering the voices of liturgists like Aidan Kavanagh and the Orthodox mission theology of Alexander Schmemann. Like Davies, Senn challenges dichotomous, utilitarian approaches to the relationship between worship and mission, stating: "We should not ask how is *our* worship to be related to *our* mission, but how is the worship in which *God* participates related to *his* mission? If worship is, in fact, a part of God's mission, then there is no separation of worship and mission from God's side. Then from our side our worship is a way of participating in the mission of God, just as our witness is."[28]

Darrell Guder and *Missional Church*, a key text in recovering a missional theology, do well to draw together the formative function of the worship service without falling into the trap of making it merely functional to some other end. On the one hand, Guder emphasizes that in corporate worship

---

26. J. G. Davies, *Worship and Mission* (London: SCM, 1966), 111.

27. Frank C. Senn, *The Witness of the Worshiping Community: Liturgy and the Practice of Evangelism* (New York: Paulist, 1993), 5. Indicating ways in which worship is an aspect of the mission of God is precisely what Davies was doing thirty years earlier. In fact, when Senn attempts to address ways in which the Eucharist is related to the mission of God, he uses Davies' construction of the relationship between baptism and Eucharist and their missionary accents to make his point (76-90).

28. Senn, *The Witness*, 88.

Christ nurtures us to live as his witnesses. On the other hand, since the
church is an *ekklesia*, a public assembly, worship *is* a public witness. In fact,
in a missional church, "worship is its first form of mission."[29]

Schattauer, building on the instincts of Davies, Senn, and Guder, further conceptualizes the relationship between worship and mission. He develops a typology for understanding past approaches that have attempted
to affirm the relationship between worship and mission and, in response
to Davies' work, offers an "inside-out" approach that "locates the liturgical
assembly itself within the arena of the missio Dei." As Schattauer explains,
"The focus is on God's mission toward the world, to which the church witnesses and is drawn, rather than on specific activities of the church undertaken in response to the divine saving initiative."[30]

Following this impulse, missional theology avoids separating the act
and being of God. That is to say, the missionary impulse is part of who God
is and not a second movement that can be differentiated from his being.
Therefore, missional theology also seeks to avoid the opposition between
what some consider the inner and outer life of the church, worship and
mission. In fact, the practices discussion is well situated to help missional
theology to articulate that the worship and witness of the church, the
greatest inherent good or intrinsic value of the practices, is bound to their
relationship to the missionary God whose glory and mission they serve.[31]

Toward an Extended Conversation:
Conclusions and Concessions

So far I have answered most of the questions raised at the beginning of this
book: I have communicated my understanding of missional theology and

29. Darrell L. Guder et al., eds., *Missional Church: A Vision for the Sending of the Church in North America* (Grand Rapids: Eerdmans, 1998), 242-43.

30. Thomas H. Schattauer, "Liturgical Assembly as Locus of Mission," in *Inside Out*, 3.

31. Dorothy Bass explains, "It has seemed to us, therefore, that to be called 'Christian' a practice must pursue a good beyond itself, responding to and embodying the self-giving dy-
namics of God's own creating, redeeming, and sustaining grace." She clarifies in a footnote,
"The 'goods' that concern us are not 'internal' to a practice but are oriented to God and
God's intentions for all creation." Bass's statement represents a welcome departure from
MacIntyre's framework. Dorothy C. Bass, "Ways of Life Abundant," in *For Life Abundant*, 30
and n. 11, respectively.

explained its antecedents. I have described how Christian practices have been understood to this point and have suggested how a missional theological perspective challenges the inner dynamics of Christian practices. What remains to be done is to explain in what ways a missional perspective changes the way that practices function in the congregation and to reflect on what Christian practices might be added to the *Practicing Our Faith* catalogue if the perspective of missional theology were adopted.

The multicultural and broad ecumenical perspective of missional theology is not well represented in the *Practicing Our Faith* literature. The world in which we are called to practice Christianity has changed; in Amos Yong's analysis we live in a "multi-religious, postmodern, and post-9/11" world.[32] Certain aspects of this changing world are addressed with different degrees of depth in *Practicing Our Faith*, as we have surveyed. What does not seem to be acknowledged by the contemporary practices discussion is that the Christianity we are called to practice is changing as well. Since World War II the center of Christianity has shifted southward, geographically and culturally, away from Europe and North America to Latin America, Africa, and southern Asia. Philip Jenkins has summarized the shift: "If we want to visualize a 'typical' contemporary Christian, we should think of a woman living in a village in Nigeria or in a Brazilian *favela*."[33] According to Jenkins, the new Christianity is more "Pentecostal,"[34] by which Jenkins means a religiosity expressed in terms of enthusiasm, fundamentalism, biblical literalism, social and moral conservatism, and is oriented toward the supernatural. The churches in the "Third World" are gaining adherents because they are providing refuge, community, and a sense of family during times of confusing social change. Furthermore, according to Jenkins, this religiosity will not be content to remain in the South. This new Christianity is being transplanted and propagated in the West by the dual forces of immigration and evangelism. Finally, the Christians in Asia and Africa, particularly, have had the expe-

---

32. Amos Yong, *Hospitality and the Other: Pentecost, Christian Practices, and the Neighbor* (Maryknoll, N.Y.: Orbis, 2008), 158.

33. Philip Jenkins, *The Next Christendom: The Coming of Global Christianity* (Oxford and New York: Oxford University Press, 2002), 2. See also the excellent summary of this shift in Dana L. Robert, "Shifting Southward: Global Christianity Since 1945," *International Bulletin of Missionary Research* 24, no. 2 (April 2000).

34. Several people have justifiably critiqued Jenkins's imprecise use of the term "Pentecostal."

rience of coexisting as religious minorities. Certainly this fact has had consequences for how they witness to God's redemptive work in their context.

Ecumenical dialogue, therefore, is an important practice for the missional theologian. Inviting Christians from other traditions into the practices conversation will expose some blind spots in the contemporary practices conversation and likely bring to the fore some other important practices for living a faithful Christian life of witness in the twenty-first century. For example, Samuel Escobar has made the point that Latin America, for so long the target of North American missionary activity, is now a growing base for missionary activity to other parts of the world.[35] I could not imagine these Christians not including *evangelism* as an essential practice of the church. But it is not enough to add an unexamined practice of evangelism to our list of Christian practices. We must ask questions like, "What could we learn about the practice of evangelism from Christians in Sri Lanka where Christians are a minority to Buddhists and Hindus and are in the midst of an ethnic and religious civil war?" In this situation evangelism would not occur out of a "centrist ecclesial identity (as in the Christendom era) but out of a marginal and ambiguous status (as in our post-colonial and post-Christendom situation)."[36] Such reflection will help us to be more faithful in our practice of evangelism in our own post-Christendom setting.

Amos Yong, in fact, could be considered the ideal missional theologian to lead such a discussion. As a theologian and clergyman with the Pentecostal Assemblies of God who was born and spent his early childhood near Kuala Lumpur, Malaysia, he embodies the new Christianity. He is attuned to the ongoing interplay between gospel, church, and culture and operates theologically out of a commitment to discerning God's ongoing redemptive mission in the world. His robust pneumatology will add depth to the Trinitarian missional theology that is emerging, and his multicultural and ecumenical perspective will contribute to our understanding of core Christian practices.

For example, from Yong's perspective, Pentecost opens up many tongues and, resultantly, many Christian practices. In his view, mission is

---

35. Samuel Escobar, *Changing Tides: Latin America and World Mission Today* (Maryknoll, N.Y.: Orbis, 2002), 153.

36. Yong, *Hospitality and the Other*, 3-15.

"nothing more or less than our participation in the hospitality of God,"[37] and the Christian concept of hospitality "provides a rich framework to think about how the many tongues, gifts and works of the Spirit enable and empower a wide range of Christian practices with regard to other religious traditions in general and people of other faiths in particular."[38] Through hospitable practices (evangelism, social witness, and interreligious dialogue), not only is God's hospitality extended to the world, but the church receives the hospitality of God through interaction with the other religions. Consider the parable of the Good Samaritan wherein it is the religious other who offers a revelation of the hospitality of God. In other words, not only are we "participants in the redemptive hospitality of God, even while we are conduits of this hospitality to the world";[39] we are obliged to discern the Spirit's presence and activity in people of other faiths. *Interfaith dialogue,* therefore, becomes an essential practice of the hospitable church. Yong argues that "the *poiesis* [work] of the Spirit" is also encountered through other Christian movements and "through those 'outside the church.'"[40] The many voices of Pentecost require many practices and a continuing conversion of current Christian practices.

Final Thoughts

The concept of "missional" has migrated far beyond its original usage in the Gospel and Our Culture conversation — and some would argue, beyond its original intent. At the same time, I realize that this book represents only one voice in that growing conversation. The contribution I have made, and what I have argued for and demonstrated in previous chapters, is that there have been important, historic antecedents of this conversation whose contributions must be considered. Furthermore, I have argued that the discipline of missional theology must be executed in a broad, interdisciplinary fashion in order that missional theology develops and impacts the church. I have attempted to give one example of how this can be done by engaging the contemporary practices discussion. I will conclude

37. Yong, *Hospitality and the Other*, 131.
38. Yong, *Hospitality and the Other*, 65.
39. Yong, *Hospitality and the Other*, 128.
40. Yong, *Hospitality and the Other*, 62.

with some thoughts on that interdisciplinary process. I feel well qualified to speak to such issues because this book began as a dissertation written for the history department, and one corner of the history department at that (Mission, Ecumenics and History of Religion). I used a theological discipline (missional theology) to look at an important issue in practical theology (the practices discussion), all while reflecting on my own ministry with adolescents with developmental disabilities. I contend that the broad conversation adds to the richness, nuance, and practicality of our insights about and practice of ministry.

Differences in theological method and emphasis between the missional theologian and the practical theologian, instead of being reasons to avoid contact, should be viewed as motivations for crossing departmental borders and as catalysts for fresh reflection on the ministry of the church. For example, Dykstra begins his reflection on the ministry of the church by addressing universal human needs through the lens of a Reformed theological anthropology. On the basis of his findings, he offers important insights about the nature of Christian ministry and suggests what preparation for that ministry might entail. His attentiveness to present and pressing human needs and the ways of life that address them can encourage missional theology not to become lost in ideas.

Guder, on the other hand, following Barth, begins his reflection on the ministry of the congregation with the doctrine of God and comes to certain conclusions about the missionary nature of the congregation. The discipleship of the church is not an end in itself; it leads to the apostolate. Guder's reflection on discipleship follows Barth's, who defines the Christian, *not* as one "distinguished from others by the address, reception, perception, use and enjoyment of the salvation of God given and revealed to the world by God in Jesus Christ." Instead, Barth defines the Christian as follows: "we understand by the Christian a man whom Jesus Christ has called to attachment to Himself, to His discipleship and to living fellowship with Himself, and whom, as we finally say, He has bound and indeed conjoined with Himself."[41] But this union with Christ is not the static union of a possessor of the *beneficia Christi*; it is a fellowship of apostolic action that finds expression in the witness of the Christian so that "with their whole being, action, inaction and conduct, and by word and speech,

---

41. Barth, *The Doctrine of Reconciliation*, 555. See Guder's application of Barth's concepts in Guder, *Continuing Conversion*, 120-42.

they have to make a definite declaration to other men."[42] This apostolic definition of a Christian and the Christian community, built upon the self-revelation of God as being for the world, lays the foundation for missional theology's unique contribution to the practices discussion.

Dykstra emphasized that the practices he imagined are dependent upon a community that is defined by its participation in the ongoing redemptive work of God. Similarly, I conclude that the proper ecclesiology for supporting missional Christian practices is a missional ecclesiology that recognizes the nature and purpose of the congregation. The discipleship that occurs in this congregation through being initiated into practices and through deepening participation in certain practices is transformative — yet this transformation comes by the Holy Spirit and cannot be manipulated, planned, or scheduled.[43]

The missional theologian and the practical theologian must work together to make sure congregations in North America are prepared to address and engage their post-Christendom setting. A missional theological conception of Christian practices offers a new paradigm for understanding the church's ministry in the world, since the old role of chaplain to society is no longer viable or defensible. Through missional Christian practices all members of the congregation take up their place of responsibility, as those who are strategically placed and adequately equipped to witness to the reign of God. Through participation in Christian practices that are formative and performative, congregations can practice their faith and practice witness.

---

42. Barth, *The Doctrine of Reconciliation*, 575.
43. Guder, "Biblical Formation and Discipleship," 72.

EPILOGUE

Amplifying Their Witness

People who work with youth tend to be more acutely aware of missional theological issues — especially with regard to analyzing a context and presenting the gospel within the categories of another culture (youth culture). Ministry with adolescents implicitly suggests contextual ministry in that adolescence involves a place (the social world of the school in which youth culture develops), a path (the road to social integration), and a purpose (forging an identity). With regard to missional theology's cross-cultural emphasis, most teens are "connected" to the larger world via the Internet and social networks. Working with adolescents means being cognizant of and attempting to understand and engage this world.

Understanding, ministering to, and practicing faith with kids who are facing the complexities of negotiating adolescence with disabilities require an even deeper degree of intentional missionary thinking. The issues I raised in the first chapter about my own ministry with adolescents with developmental disabilities, Thru the Roof, will now be addressed based on the argument made in the intervening chapters. It is now time to answer the question of specifically how missional theology's gospel, church, and culture triad helps us to address the issues raised by ministering to and with adolescents with special needs. Is there some way that the purpose of the church is particularly evident in the way we practice the faith together? How does missional theology shape our practice of the faith at Thru the Roof?

Dykstra's notion of practices, which I have found so useful in my min-

109

istry with adolescents with special needs, is challenged by the theology associated with the disability movement and by missional theology. How
has the experience of people with disabilities been considered in the *Practicing Our Faith* discussion? What other fundamental human needs can be
drawn out when the contribution and experience of people with disabilities are considered? How do we share in the prophetic activity of Christ
and share in the proclamatory aspect of Christian practices?

If we were to apply to this line of inquiry Hunsberger's missional
theological methodology, the gospel-church-culture triad, it would reveal
other questions that help me, as one who thinks missionally, to interpret
our ministry.

From Hunsberger's conversion-encounter or gospel-culture axis, I
have emphasized that the gospel and our Christian practices must be
translated into the communicative categories of people with developmental disabilities and the gospel must offer an embodied challenge to
that culture (disability culture — or the culture created by those with disabilities) and the surrounding culture (a disabling culture). In what ways
does the gospel of disability culture demonstrate "both the universality
of the gospel message and its capacity to be witnessed to by those who
derive from the many nations, cultures, ethnicities, and languages of the
world"? How can it provide a "theological rationale for preserving the in-
tegrity of difference and otherness"?[1] In what ways does our ministry
with people with disabilities support what the missiologist calls "indigenous appropriation" and what disability advocates consider the right to
"speak for ourselves"?

In the reciprocal relationship or gospel-church axis, we recognize that
the gospel can only be understood through the lenses of a culturally conditioned church. We must consider how that church's tradition has read
the texts that provide its understanding of disability. How does a liberative
hermeneutic impact our understanding of biblical notions of disability or
challenge the way we practice our faith together or how we understand
key themes like faith or discipleship? How does a missional perspective,
informed by the concerns of people with intellectual disabilities, contribute to the authenticity and faithfulness of the church as the hermeneutic
of the gospel?

---

1. Amos Yong, *Theology and Down Syndrome: Reimagining Disability in Late Modernity*
(Waco, Tex.: Baylor University Press, 2007), 11.

Finally, the missionary encounter or church-culture axis reminds us that as the plethora of culturally distinct congregations participate together in ecumenical fellowship, the gospel is expanded toward its fullness. How has my experience of working with kids with special needs made me more attentive to the ways in which those who are very differently abled than I are encountering and responding to Jesus Christ? What do my friends who are profoundly disabled and have seeming little capacity for agency teach me about the practice of hospitality and the gospel message of the hospitality of God? What do we learn about the faithfulness of God or even the *imago Dei* that we had not considered had we not shared life together?

Following the practices way of thinking about discipleship, and viewed from a missional and disability perspective, Thru the Roof makes sure that kids with developmental disabilities are being initiated into and are becoming ongoing participants in Christian practices. However, we not only participate in Christian practices. We contribute to their continuing formation and through them witness to the reign and rule of God.

Together we honor the body as the good creation of a loving God. This means, if embodiment is central to the Christian faith, that we share vulnerability and weakness as the body of Christ. It means that we revisit regnant notions of *imago Dei*. Nancy Eisland promotes a christologically informed *imago Dei* that includes, in the resurrected Christ, the marks of the passion, or the impairments of disability. Her image of the disabled God challenges notions of the ideal body and an Edenic return to perfection.[2] Indeed, the central liturgical act of the Lord's Supper draws attention to a body that has been broken. Yong extends Eisland's insights suggesting that contrary to the biomedical definition of disability, "people with disabilities also bear the image of God just as Jesus represents the fullness of that image and its restoration to the human race."[3]

Yet even Eisland's recasting of *imago Dei* focused primarily on those with physical disabilities and appealed to an *imago Dei* that is dominated by explanations of the divine image in terms of the human faculties or human reason and will. Beings without the capacity for reason are excluded.

2. Nancy L. Eiesland, *The Disabled God: Toward a Liberatory Theology of Disability* (Nashville: Abingdon, 1994), 99. "In the resurrected Jesus Christ, they saw not that suffering servant for whom the last and most important word was tragedy and sin, but the disabled God who embodied both impaired hands and feet and pierced side and the imago Dei."

3. Yong, *Theology and Down Syndrome*, 175.

As Hans Reinders, professor of ethics and mental disability, makes clear, relationship is the main characteristic of human being. The divine image exists in the freedom to be for the other. "It is the loving Father who is addressing, it is the beloved Son who is being addressed, and it is the Spirit of love that is the address passing between them."[4] Particularly in the Son we see that truly being human means being free for the other. Reinders argues that it is misdirected to try to conceive of a human nature (the particular) and then imagine Jesus as the exemplar of human nature. Instead, Jesus is created and we are created "in him" such that we are able to participate in his life and nature.[5] The shift is from understanding *imago Dei* in terms of rationality to understanding it in terms of relationship. As Barth has famously stated, "It is not the general which comes first, but the particular. The general does not exist without this particular and cannot therefore be prior to the particular."[6] In turning to God's self-revelation in Christ for our understanding of *imago Dei*, we are led to conclude that *imago Dei* is about relationality.

Those with profound intellectual disabilities, who have no apparent capacity for agency or self-determination, can participate in the Christian practice of friendship. The friendship that we extend at Thru the Roof is not friendship in general, but is instead related to the missionary nature of God as expressed in Christ and is an extension of God's friendship. Receiving the gift of God's friendship, according to Reinders, is "a prerequisite for friendship with human beings who differ from us at what is seen as the innermost core of our being."[7] Those with profound disabilities teach us how to receive God's friendship.[8] In this way, they have an evocative witness — they evoke our friendship and give us a picture of the friendship of God. They have an iconic witness — they provide windows into kingdom living and ethics. They have a Spirit-filled witness — they have the capacity, grounded extrinsically (as it is for all of us), to be signs, instruments, and foretastes of the kingdom. Our participation in the prophetic activity of Jesus Christ does not require the capacity for self-

---

4. Hans S. Reinders, *Receiving the Gift of Friendship: Profound Disability, Theological Anthropology, and Ethics* (Grand Rapids: Eerdmans, 2008), 239.

5. Reinders, *Receiving the Gift*, 240-41.

6. Karl Barth, *The Doctrine of God*, vol. II/2 of *Church Dogmatics*, ed. G. W. Bromiley and T. F. Torrance (Edinburgh: T. & T. Clark, 1957), 602.

7. Reinders, *Receiving the Gift*, 351.

8. Reinders, *Receiving the Gift*, 321.

determination. My point is that those labeled the disabled do have a capacity. They point differently, taste differently, sound and image differently, but the Spirit whose witness they bear and the kingdom and Lord to whom they bear witness are the same.

About honoring the body, we must be cognizant of how living with an intellectual disability shapes life and identity. Is there an ideal Franklin behind the autistic one I know? I do not wish to diminish or ignore the severity of Franklin's disability, but rather to note how Franklin's range of experiences has contributed to the formation of his identity and to affirm the value of the Franklin I know. As the kids have often stated, we would not be Thru the Roof without Franklin — our witness includes his erratic motions.

Among the other practices that are vital to our ministry is hospitality, whereby we follow Block's example of being "copious" hosts. Block has talked about the experience of those with disabilities in terms of "exclusion as a way of life."[9] Thru the Roof creates a space for kids with special needs to consider their agency, ability, giftedness, and contribution to their family, friends, school, and community through the practice of hospitality and witness. We believe that kids with special needs have a gift, perspective, unbridled enthusiasm, and some significant challenges that our church and our community need to be complete. We recognize that the "strange other" bears distinctive gifts that only he or she can bring to the community.

We practice testimony at Thru the Roof and affirm every adolescent's ability to share in the testimony of the church. People with developmental disabilities have an important contribution to make to our "speech" about God. What are the requirements to be a witness? To have seen, felt, or tasted something and then been willing to respond affirmatively to it with whatever capacities God has given you. It is Franklin's bounce and Brianne's hugs. Something different is required of me. Something that contributes to, confirms, and supports the testimony offered by Franklin and Brianne — an articulation of their witness to God's transformative power in our midst. At Thru the Roof we *amplify their witness.*

Amos Yong, in his *Theology and Down Syndrome*, offers us a helpful way to talk about the process discussed above that is germane to both the prac-

---

9. Jennie Weiss Block, *Copious Hosting: A Theology of Access for People with Disabilities* (New York: Continuum, 2002), 115 and 121.

tices and the missional theology discussions. Yong advocates a pneumato-logical imagination. Drawn from the biblical account of Pentecost, the pneumatological imagination challenges us to consider the relationship between unity and diversity and alerts us to "seek out, listen to, and discern the presence and activity of the Holy Spirit" in the tongues of the disabled. Consequently, the theology of disability that he develops is a "performative theology that informs, shapes, and guides the practices of the church."[10]

We have something special to say about the church's practice of healing at Thru the Roof. We can affirm John Koenig's insight that the central image for Christian healing must be wholeness and not cure.[11] The eschatological emphasis of missional theology does not point to the day when Franklin will no longer be like Franklin because he will somehow be perfected in a way that destroys his identity. If we take time to think about it, we will realize that "normal" embodiment, what is "common human experience" or being "abled" either physically and intellectually, is only temporary. The eschatological emphasis of missional theology challenges us to look now for the ways that Franklin can participate in the practices that instantiate and embody the sign, instrument, and foretaste of the kingdom of God. We look forward to the day when everybody will be able to take in the fullness of Franklin's witness. In the words of Block, "The utter mystery of God is revealed in the variety found in the human person, all of whom are created in God's likeness and image. People with disabilities give us full access to the human condition and demand that we expand our definition of 'normal' and stop making the automatic assumption that a person with a disability is 'abnormal.'"[12]

Of utmost importance to Thru the Roof is the idea that Franklin gives the community of faith "full access to the human condition," thereby revealing something about the human as created in the *imago Dei* that would otherwise have remained beyond our ken. However, as missional theology reminds us, this new knowledge offered by the Spirit has consequences for our witness. Christian practices, which Dykstra labels habitations of the Spirit, relate very naturally to Yong's notion of

10. Yong, *Theology and Down Syndrome*, 13.

11. John Koenig, "Healing," in *Practicing Our Faith: A Way of Life for Searching People*, ed. Dorothy C. Bass (San Francisco: Jossey-Bass, 1997), 149.

12. Block, *Copious Hosting*, 85.

"pneumatological imagination." As Yong explains, "The pneumatological imagination empowers Christian witness to establish a more peaceful and just society for all people, especially those with disabilities. Because the Holy Spirit empowers human witness, I claim that the pneumatological imagination not only enables human knowing but also directs liberative human activity."[13] In line with the conclusions of missional theology, "our knowing by the Spirit is never only for knowing's sake but always correlates with the larger purposes of God's redemptive work in the world."[14]

"Nothing about us without us" is a slogan of the disability movement and the title of James Charlton's work that signals the need for a people who have been oppressed and discriminated against to recover a voice, represent and define themselves and their issues, and take on the societal structures that support their oppression.[15] To Charlton's concerns, I add the recognition that those who will never have the agency to join in his program are participants in the *imago Dei* and, equally important, that they can participate in the *missio Dei* by practicing witness. If it is true that, speaking for the adolescent with developmental disabilities and following Charlton's formula, there is "no Body of Christ without us," then at Thru the Roof we are not advocating simply a theology of access with inclusion as a "gospel mandate,"[16] we are, instead, challenging the church to embody a holistic theology of witness.

---

13. Yong, *Theology and Down Syndrome*, 14.

14. Yong, *Theology and Down Syndrome*, 14.

15. James I. Charlton, *Nothing about Us without Us* (Berkeley: University of California Press, 1998).

16. Block, *Copious Hosting*, 122.

Bibliography

Aagaard, Johannes. "Some Main Trends in Modern Protestant Missiology." *Studia Theologica* 19 (1965): 238-59.

Abraham, William J. *The Logic of Evangelism*. Grand Rapids: Eerdmans, 1989.

Ahonen, Tiina. "Antedating Missional Church: David Bosch's Views on the Missionary Nature of the Church and the Missionary Structure of the Congregation." *Swedish Missiological Themes* 92, no. 4 (2004): 573-89.

Allen, Diogenes. *Between Two Worlds: A Guide for Those Who Are Beginning to Be Religious*. Atlanta: John Knox, 1977.

Andersen, Wilhelm. *Towards a Theology of Mission: A Study of the Encounter between the Missionary Enterprise and the Church and Its Theology*. London: SCM, 1955.

————. "Further toward a Theology of Mission." In *The Theology of the Christian Mission*, edited by Gerald Anderson, 300-313. New York: McGraw-Hill, 1961.

Anderson, Gerald H. *The Theology of the Christian Mission*. New York: McGraw-Hill, 1961.

Barram, Michael. "The Bible, Mission, and Social Location: Toward a Missional Hermeneutic." *Interpretation* 61 (2007): 42-58.

Barth, Karl. "Theology and Mission in the Present Situation." Lecture given at the Brandenburg Mission Conference, Berlin, April 11, 1932 (unpublished translation by Darrell L. Guder).

————. *The Doctrine of God*. Vol. II/2 of *Church Dogmatics*. Edited by G. W. Bromiley and T. F. Torrance. Edinburgh: T. & T. Clark, 1957.

————. *The Doctrine of Reconciliation*. Vol. IV/3.2 of *Church Dogmatics*. Edited by G. W. Bromiley and T. F. Torrance. Edinburgh: T. & T. Clark, 1962.

Bass, Diana Butler. *The Practicing Congregation: Imagining a New Old Church*. Herndon, Va.: Alban Institute, 2004.

Bass, Dorothy C. "The Education and Formation of People in the Faith." Caldwell Lectures presented at Louisville Presbyterian Theological Seminary, Louisville, March 6-7, 1995.

———. Preface to *Practicing Our Faith: A Way of Life for a Searching People*, edited by Dorothy C. Bass, ix-xv. San Francisco: Jossey-Bass, 1997.

———. "What Is a Christian Practice?" September 2006. Available at http://www.practicingourfaith.org/what-Christian-practice. Accessed May 22, 2007.

———. "Ways of Life Abundant." In *For Life Abundant: Practical Theology, Theological Education, and Christian Ministry*, edited by Dorothy C. Bass and Craig R. Dykstra, 21-40. Grand Rapids: Eerdmans, 2008.

———, ed. *Practicing Our Faith: A Way of Life for a Searching People*. San Francisco: Jossey-Bass, 1997.

Bass, Dorothy C., and Craig R. Dykstra. "Christian Practices and Congregational Education in Faith." In *Changing Churches: The Local Church and the Structures of Change*, edited by Michael Warren, 247-62. Portland, Oreg.: Pastoral Press, 2000.

———, eds. *For Life Abundant: Practical Theology, Theological Education, and Christian Ministry*. Grand Rapids: Eerdmans, 2008.

Bass, Dorothy C., Craig R. Dykstra, and Robert Wuthnow. "Practicing Christian Faith." Conference sponsored by the Louisville Institute for the Study of Protestantism and American Culture presented at Louisville Presbyterian Theological Seminary, Louisville, September 25-26, 1997.

Bellah, Robert N., et al. *Habits of the Heart: Individualism and Commitment in American Life*. 1st Perennial Library ed. New York: Harper and Row, 1986.

Block, Jennie Weiss. *Copious Hosting: A Theology of Access for People with Disabilities*. New York: Continuum, 2002.

Book of Confessions: Study Edition. Part I of the Constitution of the Presbyterian Church (U.S.A.). Louisville: Geneva Press, 1996.

Bosch, David Jacobus. *Transforming Mission: Paradigm Shifts in Theology of Mission*. American Society of Missiology Series, no. 16. Maryknoll, N.Y.: Orbis, 1991.

Brown, Janet L. "HIV/AIDS Alienation: Between Prejudice and Acceptance." University of Stellenbosch, 2004.

Brownson, James V. "Speaking the Truth in Love: Elements of a Missional Hermeneutic." In *The Church between Gospel and Culture: The Emerging Mission in North America*, edited by George R. Hunsberger and Craig Van Gelder, 228-59. Grand Rapids: Eerdmans, 1996.

———. *Speaking the Truth in Love: New Testament Resources for a Missional Hermeneutic*. Christian Mission and Modern Culture. Harrisburg, Pa.: Trinity, 1998.

Busch, Eberhard. *The Great Passion: An Introduction to Karl Barth's Theology*. Grand Rapids: Eerdmans, 2004.

Cahalan, Kathleen A. "Three Approaches to Practical Theology, Theological Education and the Church's Ministry." *International Journal of Practical Theology* 9 (2005): 63-93.

Cahalan, Kathleen A., and James R. Nieman. "Mapping the Field of Practical Theology." In *For Life Abundant: Practical Theology, Theological Education, and Christian Ministry*, edited by Dorothy C. Bass and Craig R. Dykstra, 62-85. Grand Rapids: Eerdmans, 2008.

Calvin, John. *Institutes of the Christian Religion.* Edited by John T. McNeill. Translated by Ford Lewis Battles. Library of Christian Classics, vols. 20-21. Philadelphia: Westminster, 1960.

Carter, Erik W. *Including People with Disabilities in Faith Communities: A Guide for Service Providers, Families, and Congregations.* Baltimore: Paul H. Brooks, 2007.

Charlton, James I. *Nothing about Us without Us.* Berkeley: University of California Press, 1998.

Coakley, Sarah. "Deepening Practices: Perspectives from Ascetical and Mystical Theology." In *Practicing Theology: Beliefs and Practices in Christian Life,* edited by Miroslav Volf and Dorothy C. Bass, 78-93. Grand Rapids: Eerdmans, 2002.

Coalter, Milton J., John M. Mulder, and Louis B. Weeks. *The Re-forming Tradition: Presbyterians and Mainstream Protestantism.* Presbyterian Presence. Louisville: Westminster John Knox, 1992.

Davies, J. G. *Worship and Mission.* London: SCM, 1966.

Dowey, Edward A., and United Presbyterian Church in the U.S.A. *A Commentary on the Confession of 1967 and an Introduction to the Book of Confessions.* Philadelphia: Westminster, 1968.

Dykstra, Craig R. *Vision and Character: A Christian Educator's Alternative to Kohlberg.* New York: Paulist, 1981.

———. "What Is Faith? An Experiment in the Hypothetical Mode." In *Faith Development and Fowler,* edited by Craig R. Dykstra, Sharon Parks, and James W. Fowler, 45-64. Birmingham, Ala.: Religious Education Press, 1986.

———. "Reconceiving Practice." In *Shifting Boundaries: Contextual Approaches to the Structure of Theological Education,* edited by Barbara G. Wheeler and Edward Farley, 35-66. Louisville: Westminster John Knox, 1991.

———. "No Longer Strangers: The Church and Its Educational Ministry." In *Theological Perspectives on Christian Formation: A Reader on Theology and Christian Education,* edited by Jeff Astley, Leslie J. Francis, and Colin Crowder, 106-18. Leominster, U.K.: Gracewing, 1996.

———. "A Way of Life." *Initiatives in Religion: A Newsletter of the Lilly Endowment, Inc.* 5, no. 4 (Autumn 1996): 1-2.

———. "Shared Practices." *Initiatives in Religion: A Newsletter of the Lilly Endowment, Inc.* 6, no. 2 (Spring 1997): 1-2.

———. *Growing in the Life of Faith: Education and Christian Practices.* Louisville: Geneva Press, 1999; 2nd ed., Louisville: Westminster John Knox, 2005.

Dykstra, Craig, and Dorothy C. Bass, "A Theological Understanding of Christian Practices." In *Practicing Theology: Beliefs and Practices in Christian Life,* edited by Miroslav Volf and Dorothy C. Bass, 78-93. Grand Rapids: Eerdmans, 2002.

Eisland, Nancy L. *The Disabled God: Toward a Liberatory Theology of Disability.* Nashville: Abingdon, 1994.

Elias, John L. *A History of Christian Education: Protestant, Catholic, and Orthodox Perspectives.* Malabar, Fla.: Krieger, 2002.

Escobar, Samuel. *Changing Tides: Latin America and World Mission Today.* Maryknoll, N.Y.: Orbis, 2002.

Farley, Edward. *Ecclesial Man: A Social Phenomenology of Faith and Reality.* Philadelphia: Fortress, 1975.

————. *Theologia: The Fragmentation and Unity of Theological Education.* Philadelphia: Fortress, 1983.

Flett, John Graeme. "God Is a Missionary God: Missio Dei, Karl Barth, and the Doctrine of the Trinity." Ph.D. diss., Princeton Theological Seminary, 2007.

Franke, John R. *Teaching Theology from a Missional Perspective.* Available from http:www.biblical.edu/images/connect/PDFs/TeachingMissionalTheology.pdf. Accessed August 23, 2007.

Freytag, Walter, ed. *Mission Zwischen Gestern Und Morgen.* Stuttgart: Evang. Missionsverlag, 1952.

Goodall, Norman, ed. *Missions under the Cross: Addresses Delivered at the Enlarged Meeting of the Committee of the International Missionary Council at Willingen, in Germany, 1952; With Statements Issued by the Meeting.* London: Edinburgh House Press, 1953.

————. "Willingen — Milestone, Not Terminus." In *Missions under the Cross: Addresses Delivered at the Enlarged Meeting of the Committee of the International Missionary Council at Willingen, in Germany, 1952; With Statements Issued by the Meeting,* edited by Norman Goodall, 9-23. London: Edinburgh House Press; distributed in the U.S.A. by Friendship Press, New York, 1953.

Guder, Darrell L. *The Incarnation and the Church's Witness.* Christian Mission and Modern Culture. Harrisburg, Pa.: Trinity, 1999.

————. *The Continuing Conversion of the Church.* Gospel and Our Culture Series. Grand Rapids: Eerdmans, 2000.

————. "From Mission and Theology to Missional Theology." *Princeton Seminary Bulletin* 24, no. 1 (2003): 36-54.

————. "Biblical Formation and Discipleship." In *Treasure in Clay Jars: Patterns in Missional Faithfulness,* edited by Lois Barrett et al., 59-73. Grand Rapids: Eerdmans, 2004.

————. "Worthy Living: Work and Witness from the Perspective of Missional Church Theology." *Word and World* 25, no. 4 (Fall 2005): 424-32.

————. "The Nicene Marks in a Post-Christendom Church." In *Perspectives — an Online Publication of the OGA,* October 2006. Available from http://www.pcusa.org/oga/perspectives/oct06/nicene-marks.pdf. Accessed November 14, 2007.

————. "The Missio Dei: A Mission Theology after Christendom." In *News of Boundless Riches: Interrogating, Comparing, and Reconstructing Mission in a Global Era,* edited by Lalsangkima Pachuau and Max L. Stackhouse, 3-25. Delhi: ISPCK, 2007.

————. "Walking Worthily: Missional Leadership after Christendom." Payton Lectures. May 2-3, 2007. Fuller Theological Seminary.

Guder, Darrell L., et al., eds. *Missional Church: A Vision for the Sending of the Church in North America.* Grand Rapids: Eerdmans, 1998.

Hall, Douglas John. *Confessing the Faith: Christian Theology in a North American Context.* Minneapolis: Fortress, 1996.

————. "Metamorphosis: From Christendom to Diaspora." In *Confident Witness — Changing World: Rediscovering the Gospel in North America,* edited by Craig Van Gelder, 67-79. Grand Rapids: Eerdmans, 1999.

Hartenstein, Karl. "Was haben wir von Tambaram zu lernen?" In *Das Wunder der Kirche unter den Völkern der Erde: Bericht über die Weltmissions-Konferenz in Tambaram,* edited by Martin Schlunk. Stuttgart: Evangelischer Missions-Verlag, 1939.

Hastings, Thomas John. *Practical Theology and the One Body of Christ: Toward a Missional-Ecumenical Model.* Studies in Practical Theology. Grand Rapids: Eerdmans, 2007.

Hoedemaker, L. A. "The People of God and the Ends of the Earth." In *Missiology: An Ecumenical Introduction; Texts and Contexts of Global Christianity,* edited by F. J. Verstraelen, 157-71. Grand Rapids: Eerdmans, 1995.

Holmes, William Gordon. *The Age of Justinian and Theodora: A History of the Sixth Century A.D.* Vol. 2. London: G. Bell and Sons, 1907.

Hout, Michael, Andrew M. Greely, and Melissa J. Wilde. "Birth Dearth: Demographics of Mainline Decline." *Christian Century* 122, no. 20 (October 2005): 24-27.

Hunsberger, George R. *The Gospel and Our Culture* 1, no. 1 (December 1987).

————. "The Newbigin Gauntlet: Developing a Domestic Missiology for North America." In *The Church between Gospel and Culture: The Emerging Mission in North America,* edited by George R. Hunsberger and Craig Van Gelder, 3-25. Grand Rapids: Eerdmans, 1996.

————. "Network News." *Gospel and Our Culture* 2, no. 1 (June 1990).

————. "Mapping the Terrain: A Proposal." *Gospel and Our Culture* 2, no. 2 (October 1990): 1-5.

————. "Major Consultation Readied." *Gospel and Our Culture* 3, no. 2 (July 1991): 1-4.

————. "Starting Points, Trajectories, and Outcomes in Proposals for a Missional Hermeneutic: Mapping the Conversation." Unpublished working paper, 2008.

Hunsberger, George R., and Craig Van Gelder, eds. *The Church between Gospel and Culture: The Emerging Mission in North America.* Grand Rapids: Eerdmans, 1996.

Hutchison, William R. *Errand to the World: American Protestant Thought and Foreign Missions.* Chicago: University of Chicago Press, 1987.

Jenkins, Philip. *The Next Christendom: The Coming of Global Christianity.* Oxford and New York: Oxford University Press, 2002.

Jones, L. Gregory. "Forgiveness." In *Practicing Our Faith: A Way of Life for a Searching People,* edited by Dorothy C. Bass, 133-48. San Francisco: Jossey-Bass, 1997.

Jones, Serene. "Graced Practices: Excellence and Freedom in the Christian Life." In *Practicing Theology: Beliefs and Practices in Christian Life,* edited by Miroslav Volf and Dorothy C. Bass, 51-77. Grand Rapids: Eerdmans, 2002.

Kelley, Dean M. *Why Conservative Churches Are Growing: A Study in Sociology of Religion.* New York: Harper and Row, 1972.

Koenig, John. "Healing." In *Practicing Our Faith: A Way of Life for Searching People*, edited by Dorothy C. Bass, 149-62. San Francisco: Jossey-Bass, 1997.

Kraemer, Hendrik. *The Christian Message in a Non-Christian World*. 7th ed. Grand Rapids: Kregel, 1969.

Lathrop, Gordon W. "Liturgy and Mission in the North American Context." In *Inside Out: Worship in an Age of Mission*, edited by Thomas H. Schattauer, 201-12. Minneapolis: Fortress, 1999.

Latourette, Kenneth Scott. *A History of the Expansion of Christianity*. Vol. 4. 7 vols. New York: Harper and Brothers, 1937.

Loder, James E. "Negation and Transformation: A Study in Theology and Human Development." In *Toward Moral and Religious Maturity*, edited by Christine Brusselmans, 165-92. Morristown, N.J.: Silver Burdett Co., 1980.

McCormack, Bruce. "Grace and Being: The Role of God's Gracious Election in Karl Barth's Theological Ontology." In *The Cambridge Companion to Karl Barth*, edited by John Webster, 92-110. Cambridge: Cambridge University Press, 2000.

MacIntyre, Alasdair C. *After Virtue: A Study in Moral Theory*. 2nd ed. Notre Dame, Ind.: University of Notre Dame Press, 1984.

Mackay, John Alexander. *A Preface to Christian Theology*. James Sprunt Lectures, 1940. London: Nisbet and Co., 1942.

———. "With Christ to the Frontier." In *Renewal and Advance: Christian Witness in a Revolutionary World*, edited by Charles W. Ranson and International Missionary Council, 198-205. London: Edinburgh House Press, 1948.

———. "The Christian Mission at This Hour." In *The Ghana Assembly of the International Missionary Council, 28th December, 1957 to 8th January, 1958; Selected Papers, with an Essay on the Role of the I.M.C*, edited by International Missionary Council and Ronald Kenneth Orchard, 100-124. London: Edinburgh House Press, 1958.

———. *Ecumenics: The Science of the Church Universal*. Englewood Cliffs, N.J.: Prentice-Hall, 1964.

McKim, Donald K. "Eschatology, Collective." In *Westminster Dictionary of Theological Terms*. Louisville: Westminster John Knox, 1996.

Matthey, Jacques. "Missiology in the World Council of Churches: Update; Presentation, History, Theological Background and Emphases of the Most Recent Mission Statement of the World Council of Churches." *International Review of Mission* 90, no. 359 (October 2001): 427-43.

Moltmann, Jürgen. *The Church in the Power of the Spirit: A Contribution to Messianic Ecclesiology*. Minneapolis: Fortress, 1993.

Neill, Stephen. *Creative Tension*. London: Edinburgh House Press, 1959.

Neill, Stephen, Gerald H. Anderson, and John Goodwin. *Concise Dictionary of the Christian World Mission*. World Christian Books. Nashville: Abingdon, 1971.

Newbigin, J. E. Lesslie. *The Household of God: Lectures on the Nature of the Church*. London: SCM, 1953.

———. *One Body, One Gospel, One World: The Christian Mission Today*. London: International Missionary Council, 1959.

————. "Ecumenics: The Science of the Church Universal." *Princeton Seminary Bulletin* 59 (1965): 60-62.

————. *The Gospel in a Pluralist Society*. Grand Rapids: Eerdmans, 1989.

————. *A Word in Season: Perspectives on Christian World Missions*. Grand Rapids: Eerdmans, 1994.

Noll, Mark A. *The New Shape of World Christianity: How American Experience Reflects Global Faith*. Downers Grove, Ill.: IVP Academic, 2009.

Olin, John C., ed. *A Reformation Debate: John Calvin and Jacopo Sadoleto*. Grand Rapids: Baker, 1976.

Osmer, Richard R. *Practical Theology: An Introduction*. Grand Rapids: Eerdmans, 2008.

Presbyterian Church (U.S.A.), Theology and Worship Ministry Unit, and Presbyterian Church (U.S.A.), General Assembly. *Growing in the Life of Christian Faith: Commended to the Church for Information and Study*. Louisville: Theology and Worship Ministry Unit, Presbyterian Church (U.S.A.), 1989.

Reeves, Thomas C. *The Empty Church: The Suicide of Liberal Christianity*. New York: Free Press, 1996.

Reinders, Hans S. *Receiving the Gift of Friendship: Profound Disability, Theological Anthropology, and Ethics*. Grand Rapids: Eerdmans, 2008.

Richardson, Cyril C., ed. *Early Christian Fathers*. Library of Christian Classics, vol. 1. New York: Touchstone, 1996.

Richter, Don Carl. "Christian Nurture in Congregations: Ecclesial Practices as Social Means of Grace." Ph.D. diss., Princeton Theological Seminary, 1992.

Robert, Dana L. "Shifting Southward: Global Christianity Since 1945." *International Bulletin of Missionary Research* 24, no. 2 (April 2000): 50-58.

Roof, Wade Clark, and William McKinney. *American Mainline Religion: Its Changing Shape and Future*. New Brunswick, N.J.: Rutgers University Press, 1987.

Rosin, H. H. *Missio Dei: An Examination of the Origin, Contents, and Function of the Term in Protestant Missiological Discussion*. Leiden: Inter-university Institute for Missiological and Ecumenical Research, 1972.

Roxburgh, Alan. "The Missional Church." *Theology Matters: A Publication of Presbyterians for Faith, Family and Ministry* 10, no. 4 (September/October 2004): 1-5.

Roxburgh, Alan J., and M. Scott Boren. *Introducing the Missional Church: What It Is, Why It Matters, How to Become One*. Grand Rapids: Baker, 2009.

Sanneh, Lamin O. *Translating the Message: The Missionary Impact on Culture*. American Society of Missiology Series, no. 13. Maryknoll, N.Y.: Orbis, 1989.

Schattauer, Thomas H. "Liturgical Assembly as Locus of Mission." In *Inside Out: Worship in an Age of Mission*, edited by Thomas H. Schattauer, 1-21. Minneapolis: Fortress, 1999.

————, ed. *Inside Out: Worship in an Age of Mission*. Minneapolis: Fortress, 1999.

Scherer, James A. *Gospel, Church, and Kingdom: Comparative Studies in World Mission Theology*. Minneapolis: Augsburg, 1987.

————. "Mission Theology." In *Toward the Twenty-First Century in Christian Mission: Essays in Honor of Gerald H. Anderson, Director, Overseas Ministries Study Center, New Haven,*

Connecticut, Editor, International Bulletin of Missionary Research, edited by Gerald H. Anderson, James M. Phillips, and Robert T. Coote, 193-202. Grand Rapids: Eerdmans, 1993.

Senn, Frank C. *The Witness of the Worshiping Community: Liturgy and the Practice of Evangelism.* New York: Paulist, 1993.

Shivute, Tomas. *The Theology of Mission and Evangelism in the International Missionary Council from Edinburgh to New Delhi.* Helsinki: Finnish Society for Missiology and Ecumenics, 1980.

Simpson, J. A., E. S. C. Weiner, and Oxford University Press. *The Oxford English Dictionary.* 20 vols. 2nd ed. New York: Clarendon, 1989.

Skreslet, Stanley H. "Nexus: The Place of Missiology in the Theological Curriculum." *Association of Presbyterians in Cross-Cultural Mission Newsletter,* no. 31 (April 1998): 1-3.

———. "Configuring Missiology: Reading Classified Bibliographies as Disciplinary Maps." *Mission Studies* 23, no. 2 (2006): 171-201.

Smith, Claire Annelise. "Foundations for Missional Christian Education." Ph.D. diss., Union Theological Seminary and Presbyterian School of Christian Education, 2005.

Stone, Bryan P. *Evangelism after Christendom: The Theology and Practice of Christian Witness.* Grand Rapids: Brazos, 2007.

Sundermeier, Theo. "Missio Dei Today: On the Identity of Christian Mission." *International Review of Mission* 92, no. 367 (2003): 560-78.

Swinton, John. "The Body of Christ Has Down's Syndrome: Theological Reflections on Vulnerability, Disability, and Graceful Communities." *Journal of Pastoral Theology* 13, no. 2 (Fall 2003): 66-78.

Van Dyk, Leanne. "The Formation of Vocation — Institutional and Individual." In *The Scope of Our Art: The Vocation of the Theological Teacher,* edited by L. Gregory Jones and Stephanie Paulsell, 225-39. Grand Rapids: Eerdmans, 2002.

Van Engen, Charles Edward. *Mission on the Way: Issues in Mission Theology.* Grand Rapids: Baker, 1996.

Verkuyl, Johannes. *Contemporary Missiology: An Introduction.* Grand Rapids: Eerdmans, 1978.

Vicedom, Georg F. *Missio Dei: Einführung in eine Theologie der Mission.* Munich: C. Kaiser, 1958.

———. *The Mission of God: An Introduction to a Theology of Mission.* St. Louis: Concordia, 1965.

Volf, Miroslav, and Dorothy C. Bass, eds. *Practicing Theology: Beliefs and Practices in Christian Life.* Grand Rapids: Eerdmans, 2002.

Walls, Andrew F. "The American Dimension of the Missionary Movement." In *The Missionary Movement in Christian History: Studies in the Transmission of Faith,* 221-40. Maryknoll, N.Y.: Orbis, 1996.

———. "Culture and Coherence in Christian History." In *The Missionary Movement in Christian History: Studies in the Transmission of Faith,* 16-25. Maryknoll, N.Y.: Orbis, 1996.

————. "The Gospel as Prisoner and Liberator of Culture." In *The Missionary Movement in Christian History: Studies in the Transmission of Faith*, 3-15. Maryknoll, N.Y.: Orbis, 1996.

————. "Missionary Societies and the Fortunate Subversion of the Church." In *The Missionary Movement in Christian History: Studies in the Transmission of Faith*, 241-54. Maryknoll, N.Y.: Orbis, 1996.

Warneck, Gustav. *Evangelische Missionslehre: Ein Missionstheoretischer Versuch.* 3 vols. Gotha: F. A. Oerthes, 1897-1903.

Weber, Otto. *Karl Barth's "Church Dogmatics": An Introductory Report on Volumes 1:1 to 3:4.* Translated by Arthur C. Cochrane. Philadelphia: Westminster, 1953.

Wilson, Jonathan R. *Living Faithfully in a Fragmented World: Lessons for the Church from MacIntyre's "After Virtue."* Christian Mission and Modern Culture. Harrisburg, Pa.: Trinity, 1997.

————. *Why Church Matters: Worship, Ministry, and Mission in Practice.* Grand Rapids: Brazos, 2006.

Winn, Albert Curry. *A Sense of Mission: Guidance from the Gospel of John.* Philadelphia: Westminster, 1981.

"Work Group Agendas (I)." *Gospel and Our Culture* 5, no. 3 (September 1993): 7.

Wuthnow, Robert. *The Restructuring of American Religion: Society and Faith Since World War II.* Studies in Church and State. Princeton: Princeton University Press, 1988.

————. *After Heaven: Spirituality in America Since the 1950s.* Berkeley: University of California Press, 1998.

Yong, Amos. *Theology and Down Syndrome: Reimagining Disability in Late Modernity.* Waco, Tex.: Baylor University Press, 2007.

————. *Hospitality and the Other: Pentecost, Christian Practices, and the Neighbor.* Maryknoll, N.Y.: Orbis, 2008.

Index

Barram, Michael, 40-42
Barth, Karl, 18, 26, 29, 106; Brandenburg lecture and *missio Dei*, 31-32; Dykstra's use of, 75, 80, 83; Guder's use of, 34-39; on vocation, 67, 95
Bass, Dorothy, 45-47; tradition as an argument, 57; use of MacIntyre, 52-53
Bosch, David, 18, 28; hermeneutics, 40; on *missio Dei*, 31-33; on the Reformation and mission, 66
Brownson, James, 40-42

Cahalan, Kathleen, 48-49, 89-90
Calvin, John, 63, 65-66, 88n.2
Christendom, 27-29, 28n.52, 33, 37, 45, 47-49, 54, 66, 73, 104, 107
Christian practices: as arenas or spaces, 3, 59, 88, 97; Dykstra's approach to, 70-78; early discussion at Lilly, 47-48; Guder's approach to, 12; Hunsberger's approach to, 13; as a means of grace, 60; missional definition of, 94; and *Practicing Our Faith*, 5n.5, 50-56; six aspects of, 56-61; worship paradigmatic of, 61-62

Discipleship: Dykstra and, 51, 55, 72, 83, 89-90, 96; with kids with disabilities, 3, 5-6, 109-15; and missional theology, 18
Disestablishment, 14, 44-45, 48
Dykstra, Craig: on Christian education, 82-85; theology of Christian practices, 70-78; use of MacIntyre, 52, 74, 76-77; on worship, 61-62

Ecclesiology: Barth critique of Protestant, 36; Dykstra on, 70, 79-82; mainline decline, 45; marks of the church, 78-79, 96; missional ecclesiology, 29, 39n.100, 107; in Westminster Confession, 23
Ecumenical, 7, 17, 23, 30, 36, 41, 71; Bosch's ecumenical paradigm of mission theology, 31; ecumenical dialogue, 103-4

Faith: challenges modern definition of, 3-4, 70; and doubt, 59, 81; Dykstra definition of, 8, 73, 97; and epistemology, 72; faith formation, 3, 85, 88,

92; and faith-world, 82; other faiths,
104-5; and mission, 80; Reformed
faith, 7, 63, 74
Farley, Edward: clerical paradigm, 48,
70-71; *ecclesia*, 70, 75, 78n.27, 81-82, 91;
"nasty suspicion," 59n.55
Flett, John, 38-39
Fowler, James, 71, 73
Franke, John, 26-27

Gospel and Our Culture Network
(GOCN), 13-18; statement of purpose,
15
Guder, Darrell: clerical paradigm,
48n.22; missional hermeneutic, 4;
and missional theology, 18-391

Hall, Douglas John, 45
Hartenstein, Karl, 24, 32
Hastings, Thomas John, 18, 91
Hunsberger, George: missional herme-
neutic, 42; missional theology, 13-18;
Newbigin triad, 15-17, 110-11
Hutchinson, William, on nineteenth-
century American mission, 21n.27

International Missionary Council
(IMC): Ghana, 29n.54; Whitby,
30n.58; Willingen, 30-32

Jones, Serene, 63-67, 94-95

Kohlberg, Lawrence, 71-72

Loder, James, 2

MacIntyre, Alasdair, 49; critique of his
conception of a social practice, 53-55,
74, 76-77; definition of social practice, 52
Mackay, John, 28-29nn.52-54; Newbigin
critique of, 93n.18

Marks of the church. *See* Ecclesiology
Missio Dei, 7, 12, 30; Bosch on, 31-33;
Flett on, 38-39; Guder on, 29-34
Missiology: definition of, 19-20n.20;
first modern missiology text, 20
Missional church, 7, 8, 10, 12, 28, 43, 67,
75, 88-89, 96; Barth's influence on,
34-38; Bosch's influence on, 33; in
doctrine of God, 101; justification for,
as response to Newbigin, 18; and
worship, 101-2
Missional hermeneutics, 40-42
Missional theology, 6, 9; definition of,
11, 39, 24-29
Mission theology (theology of mission), 3, 23-24, 28-29, 31, 101; Bosch's
ecumenical paradigm of, 31; definition of, 24; Mackay on, 29n.54

Newbigin, Lesslie: church as "hermeneutic of the gospel," 17;
Hunsberger's Newbigin triad, 15-17;
impact on Guder's missional theology, 18; impact on Hunsberger's
missional theology, 13n.1; on missions and church, 20, 92-93; participation in Christ, 7

Osmer, Richard, 4, 18

Practical theology, 4-6, 43, 89-91; as
background and setting for practices
discussion, 44-50; Dykstra's critique
of, 52, 70, 76-77; missional theology
as, 18, 39; Osmer's approach to, 4-5,
5n.6; Swinton's definition of, 4n.3

Reinders, Hans, 112

Sanneh, Lamin, 16, 91n.13
Smith, Claire, 84-85
Swinton, John, 4n.3

Vocation, 11, 26, 28, 34, 39, 66-67, 94-96, 98; Barth on, 35, 37, 67, 95

Walls, Andrew, 16-17; on American frontier missions, 21-22, 58, 58n.51
Warneck, Gustav, 20

Worship: missional approach to, 99-102; in *Practicing Our Faith* discussion, 61-62

Yong, Amos, 103-5, 113-14